author of
from beyond the skies

juli boit

brave

love

A Nurse's Story of Courage and Compassion in a Kenyan Hospice

Published by hope*books
2217 Matthews Township Pkwy
Suite D302
Matthews, NC 28105
www.hopebooks.com

hope*books is a division of hope*media network

Printed in the United States of America by hope*books

First paperback edition.
Paperback ISBN: 979-8-89185-006-4
Hardcover ISBN: 979-8-89185-012-5
Ebook ISBN: 979-8-89185-007-1
Library of Congress Number: 2023916753

Cover design by Drew Shafer

All Bible references use King James Version of the Bible Modern English Version unless otherwise stated.

hope*books
hopebooks.com
Because the world needs your hope-filled
words now more than ever

For Titus and our beloved children

Table of Contents

The Shelter of Each Other

There is a small village in western Kenya, just north of the equator, where the sun rises and sets at the same time year round. Sun-friend, as my little boy Geoffrey calls it, is ushered in 365 mornings a year by the singing of a choir of birds. Stubbornly hopeful, they sing of new mercies available for the day in a world that seems as beautiful as it is broken. A world where my son asks how to spell "hunger," "puppy," and "Lego," all in one list.

For nearly two decades, this village—filled with its rolling green hills and a river through its center—has been my home. Its red dirt roads hold my footprints as well as those of my neighbors who have welcomed me and allowed me to belong here. The wisdom of their way of life has taught me over and again: "A person becomes a person through other people."

No doubt, I am who I am because of the people—my family, friends, patients, colleagues, and neighbors—who have allowed me to walk alongside them while teaching me about hope, resilience, and hospitality. These are the

1

people who have been patient with me as I continue to grow in the ways of love and faith.

I am who I am because of the people who have chosen to accompany me, affirming my worth beyond anything I accomplish, own, or do. People who have helped me back up after I fall. People with whom we've celebrated moments of victory, both big and small, through singing and dancing, through the sharing of a plate of vegetables and *ugali*—the staple cornmeal cake of Kenya. People I've sat with in silence, and they with me, as we mourned death and disappointment.

And, remarkably, they are who they are because of me, too. In all our diversity and likenesses, in our strengths and weaknesses, in joy and sorrow, we are bound together because we are loved by God.

In 2004, I moved from Los Angeles to this village, Kipkaren River. I was a single, twenty-five-year-old nurse practitioner with three years of experience working in an HIV unit in L.A., aware of the AIDS crisis in Kenya affecting mostly young adults and children. At the time, the villages in Kenya had access to neither HIV testing nor treatment, and the stigma and fear that accompanied the disease was untellable.

I left my home and family in California and moved to Kenya for what I thought would be a year or two. I had visited Kipkaren during nursing school trips starting in the summer of 2000 and had witnessed the devastation of HIV/AIDS within the community. During those trips, I worked in a small nonprofit organization and became friends with remarkable Kenyan leaders who cared deeply about the suffering of their people. They invited me to come and be a part of their HIV home-based care program that was just beginning. One year stretched to two, which turned into five years of listening, learning, and loving as I worked alongside Kenyan colleagues, dreaming of ways to serve our patients and the larger community.

That dreaming turned into a reality in 2009 when I founded Living Room International to meet the holistic needs of seriously ill adults and children and to provide life-giving and transformative refuge for thousands of people in Kenya.

This collection of stories is inspired by nearly twenty years of living and working among the people of Kenya. It is held together by the common theme of what it looks like to love with courage and compassion in community. I think of these stories as threads woven together into the fabric of who I am, of who I am still becoming.

Likewise, though each piece on its own comprises a set of meaningful moments and memories, the threads interlace to form the beautiful, diverse tapestry that is community.

There's an Irish proverb that says, "It is in the shelter of each other that a person lives." It is in such shelter, in community, that I have been shaped into a more compassionate, brave person. Transforming the lens through which I see the world, it also undoubtedly plays a part in how I tell these stories.

As a Christian, wrestling with issues of justice and poverty and what it might look like to participate in the disparities that exist in my neighborhood.

As a nurse, advocating for patients to have access to quality, affordable healthcare services.

As a wife of a Kenyan man and a mother to black and brown children who came to our family both biologically and through adoption.

As a mama who has experienced the personal trauma of my own children's battles with devastating illness.

From these vantage points, I contemplated and wrote these stories.

Toward the end of writing this manuscript, I reached a point where I no longer felt up to the task. Overwhelmed with doubt, I laid on my bed and had a full on, out loud, heart-to-heart conversation with myself, trying to summon the gumption to finish it.

My mind echoed the title of a poem by Sean Thomas Dougherty, "Why Bother?" I copied it in black Sharpie on a three-by-five index card taped to my desk. It sits just above my computer, at eye level, serving as a reminder of the reason I write these words that now fill this book. Below the title's question, the hand-copied poem holds the answer.

Because right now,

there is someone out there with

a wound in the exact shape

of your words.[1]

Writing this book has been a labor of love, an invitation to remember and notice, to feel once again the joy and pain, the wonder and the sorrow of this journey. It is my account, though I recognize it's not solely my own to tell.

Honoring the lives of the people who play a part in these stories feels deeply important to me, and I endeavored to reflect the beauty and complexity of the

---

1 Sean Thomas Dougherty, *The Second O of Sorrow* (Rochester: BOA Editions Ltd., 2018), 9.

people I've come to love and the life I've been blessed to live in Kenya.

My hope is that you'll hear in these stories an invitation, an assurance that there are opportunities for all of us to grow in the ways of love. We find them within our homes and our neighborhoods, as well as within ourselves. And as we are willing to listen and learn from one another, face our fears, see injustice, and leave room for God to interrupt our plans, we will grow in the courage and compassion it takes to say "yes" to what love asks of us.

It's a story about returning
to a place, a people, a time.
We were not the same
but welcomed still.

It's a story about returning,
weary and worn, wonder filled
with sounds of singing
ushering us home.

It's a story about returning,
fragile new life found in the dark.
The shelter of love held.
The scars left by the healing.

Chapter One

Coming Home

I crawled under the canopy of a mosquito net to sleep in my own bed for the first time in 481 days. Beyond spent from the never-ending day of flights spanning the globe, my husband and four little ones, also exhausted, preceded me to sleep. We had flown from Los Angeles to Paris to Nairobi to Eldoret, and made the final two-hour drive from Eldoret to the village of Kipkaren River where our family lives.

A serenade of insects outside my window quieted the host of thoughts filling my mind. *We got to come home, all of us.* This had been the plan when we left Kenya to head to Los Angeles for our boys to undergo bone marrow transplants, but then the complications mounted, and death came nearer than we'd ever imagined. The notion of us surviving, of there being a full recovery, of all six of us returning, was slippery to hold onto for so many days. But here we were.

There's no place like home, the old saying goes. But what happens when you return to a beloved place and you're no longer the same—marked by equal parts trauma and wonder?

Suleika Jaouad writes, "It's a funny thing, coming home. Everything smells the same, looks the same, feels the same, but you are different; the contrast between who you were when you left and who you are now is heightened against the backdrops of old haunts."[2]

I left Kenya in September of 2017 thinking our children's treatment and recovery would be difficult but manageable. We'd go and get it done within a few months and return home with cured children and a good, redemptive story. I'd keep up on work emails and attend meetings, day and night, by phone from hospital hallways. And while our boys were being healed, our Living Room team would construct a forty-nine-bed hospital that would be ready to open by the time we got home. I'd jump right back in where I had left off.

I look back on my expectations versus the reality of our experience like those Pinterest fail photos.

I had followed instructions and done my best, but most days felt unscripted, like the wildest ride of our lives. The boys (eventually) were cured, but the road

2 Suleika Jaouad, *Between Two Kingdoms: A Memoir of a Life Interrupted* (New York: Random House, 2021), 42.

getting there was messy and left all of us scarred. We (eventually) came home—after one failed attempt, a year or so later than expected.

I wrote emails and attended phone meetings (most of the time), but I also desperately needed help and required rest along the way. Our Living Room team did indeed construct a hospital that was ready to open, and we were now back in Kenya and excited to be a part of it.

The problem was, I couldn't jump right back in as if nothing had happened or changed within me.

Twice, I had witnessed death and new life. The memories were still fresh. On the days leading up to Christmas of 2017, I had sat in a cold ICU room and listened as machines rattled and hissed to breathe for our beloved nineteen-month-old baby.

With a perpetual tear-stained face, I prayed wordless prayers as one horrifying complication mounted on top of the next, threatening to steal our child. And when, thankfully, Ryan didn't die, I hardly had time to process it, as some one hundred days later, long before he had recovered, we faced another bone marrow transplant for three-year-old Geoffrey.

It was too soon. Too overwhelming. Too much.

The experience gutted me, leaving me more tender and awe-filled than I'd ever been.

I had reached, over and again, what felt like the end of my limits while still more was required. In the most beautiful of ways, community filled in so many gaps. But the rebirth of our boys didn't erase the suffering they had endured, nor did it heal the trauma in all of us. The chronic stress of our bodies and minds sensing more signs of danger than safety for months on end took a toll.

* * *

Due to the nature of our work, a documentary team followed our family's transplant journey from Kenya to Los Angeles, throughout the numerous hospital stays, and then back to Kenya. They traveled ahead of us to film our village welcoming us home, capturing the exuberant singing and dancing and a host of familiar faces gathering to receive us.

The images document how tired and relieved we were to step back onto our red dirt road, with Geoffrey and Ryan in our arms wearing matching Superman t-shirts. We're singing along with our community as we march down the path that leads toward our house.

It's dusk, and as sun-friend leaves us to go to America, I'm sitting in the dark on our porch. The camera light shines on my face, and all the emotions of the welcome ceremony are still fresh. I do an interview, my face worn-out and voice hoarse.

I don't look into the camera but at my friend, Kimberly, who sits beside it. She and her husband, Travis, have captured hundreds of hours of interviews over nearly two years. She knows me through and through and asks me what I'm feeling. I smile gently and say, "It's overwhelming to be received by a community that you know loves you in the ways that they do, that we love too. I feel like it's been a million miles to get here, but I'm so grateful to have arrived."

With tears in my eyes, I pause before continuing. "I'm always amazed by the generosity that is on display here. It is moving that so many people we love showed up. They've been waiting for us to come, and we came. All of us. There were days I didn't know if that was going to happen. As we were traveling, I felt this sense—everything we hoped for has happened. We asked for the boys to have life, and they have it."

* * *

When Living Room began in 2009, we decided to name the hospice *Kimbilio*, meaning "a place to run to; a refuge." We dreamed of creating a shelter where compassion was extended to those who needed it most.

Among the first guests to come to Kimbilio were Faith and Elizabeth. Both were my age, around thirty years old, and had lost their health and dignity, among so many other things, to HIV/AIDS. Neither could walk or speak.

When Elizabeth arrived, she had already buried both her children, and her suffering was simply too much for her to bear. For months, all she did was scream, the sound of her anguish excruciating. Our team worked day and night to provide relief for her physical, emotional, and spiritual pain.

It is hard to say what caused her screaming to stop, but one day it finally did. Maybe it was reprieve from the physical pain, acceptance that she was loved, or some sort of grace from God.

As for Faith, I first met her lying on a mattress on the grass outside a relative's home. She wore a Disney t-shirt that had somehow found its way from the US to Kenya. It showed Eeyore, a gloomy stuffed donkey, along with the words, *Thanks for noticing me.*

The Bible tells of a talking donkey, and I assure you, I heard God speaking to my soul through that Disney t-shirt, and I didn't know what to do.

I asked myself the question that so often serves as a guide when I'm unsure of what the next step is: *What does it look like to love in this situation?* Not as a way to make myself feel more comfortable with her suffering, but to pause and pay attention. To see Faith, not just her disease or disability. To notice and affirm her worth and the God whose image she bears—the image we share.

And in that act of pausing and paying attention, I found my answer. I would bring her to Kimbilio.

Over time, the transformation our team witnessed in both Elizabeth and Faith's remaining days was nothing short of miraculous. Their disease continued to be debilitating, and we grieved losses and disappointments with them along the way. In the most astounding of ways, they knew they were loved. They knew Kimbilio was a place where they were valued.

Sitting side by side on the veranda of Kimbilio Hospice, Elizabeth and Faith spent much of their days together. Their broken bodies displayed such a sense of nobility, it still brings tears to my eyes. We lovingly referred to them as the queens of Kimbilio.

* * *

When Jesus lived his thirty-three years on earth, walking dirt paths and fishing alongside his friends, he showed us who God is. He took on flesh and all its vulnerability and moved into a neighborhood. Jesus came as a baby with a first breath to be breathed, a mother's breast to nurse as a life source.

He'd grow up and speak about a kingdom coming where the poor would be included, where they would always have enough. The brokenhearted would laugh again. The blind would see. The deaf would hear. The shamed would be welcomed and begin to understand their worth.

He'd laugh over a meal shared with friends and weep with grief over a city that cared more about rules and being right than justice and mercy. Jesus would take on pain, suffering, and death, ultimately showing us there is no place God isn't willing to go for the sake of love.

Jesus often told stories about something of value being lost—a sheep, a coin, a son—that is searched for and rejoiced over when found.

I draw a lot of comfort from the words of K. J. Ramsey, who wrote, "There is no road too rocky or trail too long for God to travel to pursue and gather up the hurting parts of you. There is no part of you that is too broken, too angry, too anxious, too judgmental, too traumatized, or too lifeless for God to seek."[3]

---

3 K. J. Ramsey, *The Lord Is My Courage: Stepping Through the Shadows of Fear Toward the Voice of Love* (Grand Rapids: Zondervan Reflective, 2022), 191.

I have long known this to be true, trusting it for others like Faith and Elizabeth when they couldn't yet believe it for themselves.

For years, I've helped care for the sick and the dying and listened to orphaned children close their daily prayers by reciting these words: "Surely goodness and mercy shall follow me all the days of my life; and I will dwell in the house of the Lord forever" (Ps. 23:6).

Parts of me had been lost and broken while I was away going through the boys' treatment. What I had long believed for others I now needed to believe for myself.

* * *

Out of medical necessity, long before concepts like social distancing and shelter at home had meaning to the general public, our family lived them for fifteen months while in Los Angeles for our sons' bone marrow transplants.

We lived in and out of hospitals and leaned heavily on the kindness of a community that walked alongside us. It was our turn to wear the *Thanks for noticing me* t-shirt for a solid year. The sacrifices required for our boys to be cured—made by us and those who helped us along the way—were both costly and worth it.

Each of our children experienced those fifteen months away from home differently, and we couldn't begin to know all the ways they would continue to process them. Ryan, our youngest, had come to us just two weeks old after his mama died in childbirth. Now, at nearly two, he was cured of sickle cell disease.[4]

His brother, Geoffrey, also cured and living with us as our own, was four. My firstborn, Ella, was five, strong and bright, and vocal about the tension she felt moving from one continent to the other.

The boys' biological sister, Alice, was ten and still had sickle cell. She hadn't been able to travel with us because she didn't have a donor match in any sibling. We hadn't been able to get her guardianship application finalized prior to the trip, but now that we had come back, we worked through finding our way and rebuilding the relationships with Alice in our home and family.

The oldest of the boys' siblings to live with us was Sharon, who was thirteen. As the donor match for her brothers, she had come to California with us. She was now back in the village she knew as home, experiencing

---

4 Sickle cell disease (SCD) is an inherited red blood cell disorder. In someone who has SCD, instead of having round red blood cells that carry oxygen to all parts of the body, some red blood cells are C-shaped, like a sickle. These C-shaped cells become hard and sticky, so when they travel through small blood vessels, they get stuck and clog the blood flow. This causes pain and other serious, life-threatening problems.

a complexity of grief and loss, rediscovering who she was after being away for what felt like a lifetime.

Each one of us had experienced brokenness and loss—some of it merely inconvenient, other parts devastating in nature. But through the journey, we were also expanded and strengthened in meaningful ways.

Back home in Kenya, we all felt the need to sift through the losses and gains, to grieve as well as to recount and celebrate. One truth did not override the other. Both mattered. All felt sacred.

* * *

Ryan's play, one morning not long ago, involved him listening to my heart with a stethoscope. He clearly knew how to use it, as well as a blood pressure cuff and pulse oximeter. He fears going anywhere near a lab, as needles had been a routine part of his life since he was six months old until he was healed.

Meanwhile, Geoffrey talks about missing his doctors. He describes, as he remembers, aspects of living in the hospital, sometimes telling of the time he required oxygen and wore a face mask. "I didn't like that," he says.

And Ella? She has tried to fit all of the time we spent in the States into categories that make sense to her little mind and heart. We talk about sickle cell disease and

19

how Ryan and Geoffrey used to have it. She reasons, "Well, Sharon gave her blood to help them get better." Yes, she did.

I still wrestle with the harsh reality that Alice didn't have the opportunity for treatment like her brothers, nor to be with us for those fifteen months in the States.

* * *

As we all transitioned back into our home and work in Kenya, I walked through the village and pondered it all. *Did this really happen? Did we survive the darkness? The uncertainty?*

My emotions fluctuated day to day and moment by moment between so many polar opposites. I felt numbness and an overwhelming tenderness. I shifted between relief that it was over and we were finally home to sadness that it was finished and we were no longer around friends who had become family. I felt gratitude for the healing yet wounded by the process.

I trusted that God cared about all the parts—the ones that hurt, the buried and forgotten ones, the healing ones.

I continued a routine I had started in Los Angeles. Now, back in Kenya, I'd wake up early in the morning, long before the sun rose and my children were awake, and I'd slip into our living room where there was about a fifty-fifty chance the electricity would be off.

If it was, I'd sit and write by the light of a lantern with a cup of tea in hand, remembering the story we'd lived, letting my words rise from within—some surprising me, awakening me to the emotions attached to them. Tears would trickle and, at times, run wild.

Those writings would eventually become the book, *From Beyond the Skies*, but before they were shared with anyone else, they were my unfiltered prayers. My buried emotions to dig through and reflect upon. My losses to grieve. My joy about the wonder of how it even happened at all—how we dared to believe for medical miracles for our little boys. How we loved bravely, even though it never felt like it was enough. How vulnerable and utterly exposed I had felt, even though I knew we never walked alone.

We were home, but I wasn't ready to jump ahead, to process what might come next. Yes, there was urgent and important work to be done, but before I could engage wholeheartedly, I needed to soak in what had happened— to remember and ponder it all within my heart.

At one point or another, we must all find our way back from a grueling journey, literally or metaphorically.

Perhaps, in our pausing, we can learn that our tears are kept track of and our wholeness matters to God.

For me, I needed to lean into the beautiful community of Living Room that I had helped to create, which in turn had taught me so much of what I know about vulnerability, resilience, and compassion.

I needed to be held in the hope and love we offer to others, making space for me to begin to heal.

What if love
is at times a willingness to try,
one unsure step in front of the next?
A cup of cold water,
perhaps it's lukewarm.
An exchange, kindness. Offered, received.
A moment, if noticed,
right here and now—
mundane laced with profound mystery.

Chapter Two

The Guiding Question

Two days after arriving back in Kenya, Titus and I stepped onto the newly completed Living Room Hospital grounds in Eldoret. The beauty of the property, with its massive canopy of trees and vibrant floral gardens, had always felt like an extravagant, unexpected gift from God. Now the buildings we had meticulously planned were constructed, built while we were away.

The grounds were bigger and more lovely than I had ever imagined. I paused on the brick walking path surrounded by shades of lavender and looked around, breathing it all in. Through wonder-filled tears, I whispered to Titus, "I didn't dream this."

He grabbed my hand and simply nodded, affirming the awe we both felt.

We entered the hospital building—the smell of fresh paint hung thick in the air—and admired it room by room. In time, the space would be furnished with hospital beds and medical equipment.

When we stepped into the pediatric unit, I had trouble catching my breath for a moment, overwhelmed by the gravity I felt in the room. It would soon be filled with bald-headed, emaciated little ones and their mothers—women intimately acquainted with the anguish that accompanies parenting a critically ill child.

I didn't have to imagine the prayers they cried into the night or how gutturally painful and powerless it is to watch your child suffer deeply and not be able to protect them.

I had the muscle memory for all of it.

Although the room was still empty, I could envision the colorful quilts spread across hospital beds. I conceded to Titus, "I don't want any child to need this place. I don't want them to need hospice care at all." I looked deep into his kind, brown eyes and continued, "But when they do need it, I want us to love them well."

I wasn't ready or interested in jumping back into life and work as if nothing had happened to my children and family, and I trusted this space to be a refuge—not safe from death or suffering—but filled with immense tenderness and compassion. A place of love for me to lean into alongside the other mamas and babies who would come into it with the hope of healing.

* * *

Today, I stand at the bedside of Kiptum, an eighteen-month-old, malnourished baby, swaddled like a newborn in a pink quilted blanket and held in his exhausted mama's arms. Kiptum is HIV positive and failing to thrive due to a lack of food and treatment.

Yesterday, he was admitted to Living Room's newly opened hospital for intensive care, referred from an outpatient HIV clinic that Living Room partners with.

As our pediatrician, Dr. Esther, gently opens the blankets to reveal Kiptum's sunken frame, the little one is awake but lies still. Too still. He lacks energy to play, sit up, babble, or even cry.

The referral call could almost be scripted by this point: "We have a newly diagnosed baby who is malnourished and failing to thrive. Do you have space to care for him?"

Sometimes, we have a bed available and sometimes sadly not.

More than answering questions about the availability of beds, our team must answer the underlying questions like: Do we have room to love again, knowing the outcomes are uncertain? Will we choose to try, to give our best, even when it feels like it wouldn't be enough? Are we willing to care, knowing love is costly?

The babies come to us looking like they will not, no, *cannot* survive, but our team lovingly cares for them, time and again. Often, they've recovered in such dramatic ways in just a few weeks that they are almost unrecognizable. A combination of medical science and extreme mercy, lived out moment by moment, makes way for miracles. Not the instantaneous, "Poof and it's done!" kind, but a slower way, devoid of quick fixes or easy solutions.

The miracles we see come wrapped in a sort of patience and kindness intertwined with an awareness that there is no hurrying this sort of healing. As I would come to understand in my own healing, yes, God could speed it up, but perhaps the gradualness is part of the kindness, part of what is needed most.

Other times, a child arrives at Living Room and the prescribed formula of medicine, nutrition, and compassionate care is given, but death still comes. With it, our team rightly feels the disappointment and loss, the kind of grief that warrants wailing, the wrongness of a child's body placed in a box and buried in the ground.

In this work of loving, there's no guaranteed outcome, just a recurring invitation to love. A trust that God is with us. A conviction that every child is worth it.

Today, it is Kiptum's turn. His body is fragile. He needs nourishment, but he no longer feels hunger and has dangerously lost his drive to eat. Dr. Esther asks his mama a series of questions as she tenderly and thoroughly examines Kiptum's body, articulating her clinical findings to us, the larger care team in the room.

I recognize the angst, the fear, the desperate hope this mama feels as she watches the poking and prodding, as she struggles to answer each question.

"Mama Kiptum, when were you first diagnosed with HIV?"

Dr. Esther notes ulcers in Kiptum's mouth.

"How long has Kiptum been on medication for HIV? For his TB?"

There is pus coming from his ears; it seems he has had recurrent ear infections.

"What antibiotics is he on? We need to add vinegar rinses. How long were you able to breastfeed Kiptum? His liver is tender and enlarged. Let's repeat a liver function panel. How long has it been since he was hungry? We need to place an NG tube for his feedings since he isn't tolerating anything by mouth."

I lean in, and Kiptum's big brown eyes lock with mine. I find myself wanting to look away, but I don't. It's uncomfortable to be confronted with such brokenness and suffering in a child. But the more I look, the more I care. I whisper, "*Pole mtoto. Pole. Utapona.*" I'm sorry, little one. I am sorry. You will be healed.

The phrases may sound trite—a condolence and an impossible promise wrapped up into one. It isn't a prayer for instant recovery. Love, in this moment, demands far more than that. It's a gentle and intentional affirmation: *You are loved and worthy of it. You are loved and worthy of it.* Over and over again.

With every drop of milk: *You are loved and worthy of it.*

In every word spoken to this mother, without the shaming that life has taught her to expect: *You are loved and worthy of it.*

Tears fill my eyes, originating from some place deep within. They don't spill over but sit with me in the wonder of a seemingly ordinary moment that feels inexplicably sacred. This moment in some ways mirrors the sense of hopelessness and gratitude I felt at the bedside of my own children. The desperate need of this mama to hear words of comfort echo my own from not so long ago.

These aren't tears of pity or sadness but of understanding. It's love that moves me. Love looks exactly like this. A mama and her baby rightly seen, acknowledged, and accepted as valuable, even though the world and its systems scream that they are poor and insignificant.

This moment, somehow, holds everything that is both right and wrong in the world.

The guiding question of Living Room's work, of my life, has become this: What does it look like to love in this situation?

While it may seem cliché, reminiscent of the fluorescent WWJD?[5] rubber bracelets my church youth group wore in the 1990s, I find the question to be grounding and helpful, and not because the answer is often obvious in the moment.

Sometimes, I do know the right or wrong thing to do. But more often, the question itself is an opportunity to lean into the situation, to pay attention, to notice.

---

5 WWJD? is an abbreviation for "What would Jesus do?" It is used among some Christians as a motto to encourage behavior that is consistent with Jesus's teachings.

What is the most loving thing to do or not do? To say or not say? To cry or laugh? To sit in silence or get up and dance?

* * *

The first time I remember specifically asking this question was in 2008 after a series of home visits. It was an average Tuesday when the suffering of two little kids became too much. It wasn't so different from many of the other days during which our team had gone into the community and encountered abject poverty and crushing disease.

Regularly, we would sit alongside pain that went far beyond the physical and linked itself to the emotions and spirit of individuals and families. Almost daily, we sat in homes with grass roofs and prayed for bread, that there would somehow be enough. Sometimes, love led us to bring the food we were praying for, to bandage wounds and to hold the hands of the sick and dying.

But four years into my living in Kenya, everything changed in one afternoon. Maybe the sun was too hot as we walked the dirt paths in the village that led to the homes we visited. Or maybe all the other visits had somehow led us to this moment when discontentment with needless suffering consumed us, when we refused to accept death was inevitable. Compassion arose and prompted the question we could no longer ignore: What does it look like to love in *this* situation?

A grand tree with whitish bark stood majestically at the edge of the dirt road leading to the home of our patient, a two-and-a-half-year-old living with her grandmother. The tree's branches stretched far and wide, providing shade under its canopy of green leaves.

I stood alongside Ruth, a colleague and a friend, to rest for a moment from the sun's heat and to take a drink of water before entering the home. Some chickens freely roamed around our feet, clucking and scratching the ground in search of food.

I studied the landscape surrounding us, a stunning view across the valley filled with a thousand shades of green and brown under the bright blue sky. I was reminded of a friend's comment from long ago that when God made Kenya, He got out the big box of crayons.

We approached two mud huts and entered the smaller one, the kitchen. The smell of smoke from the fire in the corner heightened my senses. Water boiled for the preparation of a cup of afternoon chai, firewood neatly stacked overhead.

The toddler we had come to visit, a little girl named Flovia, lay alone on the kitchen floor on top of a plastic sack used for storing dried corn. She was awake but too weak to sit up or speak. Flovia, an HIV positive orphan, was on the verge of starvation.

Her grandmother did her best, she said, but felt overwhelmed by the care needed, by the degree of sickness filling Flovia's tiny frame.

I picked Flovia up and listened with my stethoscope to her heartbeat, to her lungs. I felt her distended belly and examined her stick-thin arms and swollen legs. She needed treatment that was only available far away. Or so it felt. I placed her back onto the floor and gently rubbed her back. *There must be a better way*, I thought.

Ruth and I walked in silence to our next home visit. We went a mile or so along the dirt road before turning onto a narrow *panya* route, a rat's path, as they're often referred to here. The bushes brushed us on both sides until a small opening appeared, and a mud hut sat before us.

A twenty-year-old mama named Emily had her baby, Felix, secured to her back with a brightly colored piece of fabric. Emily bent over two yellow basins filled with laundry she was washing by hand. She paused from her work to receive us and wiped the soap suds from her hands. "*Karibu*." Welcome, she said.

"*Asante.*" Thank you.

We sat down in the single-room house of Mama Felix, as she was called according to Kenyan custom. She untied the knots holding her baby to her back and carefully transferred eleven-month-old Felix's sleeping body onto her lap.

I was struck by how exhausted she looked. It had been three months since her husband died and she found out her positive HIV status. Since learning her baby had it too.

"*Habari yako?*" How are you? we asked.

Automatically, she responded, "*Mzuri.*" Fine. But nothing about the moment or her situation was fine.

Years later, I would stand in the ICU next to my child's bed and find the simple question of "How are you?" to be so big and overwhelming, it felt almost cruel. I'd answer, "Ok," unsure of what else to say.

Mama Felix was simply trying to survive. She didn't have the option—the luxury, really—to dwell on her struggles. If she were to list them, where would she even begin? And would they ever end?

She didn't hesitate to tell us about her baby's challenges, though. She was worried about his cough

35

and high fever which mostly occurred at night. She was anxious that he was losing weight, that she saw no improvement despite her faithful administration of his medications. He only got sicker.

When Felix woke up, his countenance looked much like what we had just seen on Flovia's face. Lethargic, weak, wasted. The weight in the room felt insurmountable, like there wasn't a way forward that would lead toward life.

* * *

That evening, I sat in the home of David and Allison, my dearest friends and coworkers, sharing a simple meal together. We talked about the day, about the home visits, about how these children, our neighbors, were so near death. We discussed what it might look like, logistically, to set up an inpatient feeding program for Flovia and Felix. We wondered, Could we? Should we?

Allison, the most detailed, methodical planner of us all, mercifully said, "Let's try." Agreeing to action without having a clear plan wasn't like her. But we were compelled by a bigger question: What does it look like to love?

Our journey of loving bravely started with willingness.

36

We understood "trying" meant having the courage to step into a new space that felt daunting and scary. It involved adjusting our team's plans and program to make room for these little ones' chance to live.

To be clear, "trying" was not a "better than nothing" approach. We were trained healthcare providers working within our scope of practice at a medical facility, but there still was no guaranteed outcome. These children were acutely ill, and it was obvious they weren't going to survive for more than a few days or weeks without intervention.

The next day, we consulted with pediatricians and staff at the nearby HIV treatment center about the therapeutic feeding requirements. We bought beds and bedding, basins and towels, dishes and food items. We hired Kenyan caregivers to stay with the children around the clock, and we met with Flovia's grandmother and Felix's mother.

We planned and prayed and made room.

Beyond the extensive planning and logistics required, my thoughts wrestled with the weighty responsibilities and the impossible decisions that would inevitably accompany providing inpatient care to these orphaned children on the brink of death.

It was daunting to step into the unknown—choosing to sit alongside suffering, caring in tangible ways, as we'd watch and wait without any assurance of what was to come.

Hope felt like a dangerous thing.

Love made us vulnerable.

Flovia and Felix arrived at the clinic that evening as the sun's light was fading. Ingrained in my memory is the image of Flovia, propped up on a scale. Her clothes had been removed, and the look of anguish on her face undid me.

The two-and-a-half-year-old weighed twelve pounds. Baby Felix's tiny body followed in the exercise; he was a mere nine pounds.

The work of loving began, or maybe it just entered a new phase. It would be costly, unpredictable, and, we desperately hoped, worth it. I somehow understood, though, the invitation was to love, regardless of the outcome.

Within a day of initiating specialized feedings of formula made of milk, sugar, oil, and minerals, given every two hours, I walked into the room to find Flovia sitting up in bed, holding her cup, feeding herself.

Within a week, she had regained enough strength to start toddling. And within a month, she was speaking in two languages (Kalenjin and Kiswahili) and calling all the women and men who shared in her care "Mama."

We were growing in the ways of love, and Flovia's life was showing us that, with God, nothing was impossible.

Felix's progression was less dramatic. He had trouble tolerating the formula and keeping down the necessary medications. He was sweet and so very sick. A pastor from a local church who came to visit and pray for the children picked up Felix, holding him close to his face.

As he tenderly looked at Felix and prayed for healing to come to his broken body, the tears began to flow down the pastor's face. "I see the image of God, right here and now," he said.

Six weeks into their care, while Flovia was growing and thriving, Felix went into respiratory distress. We transferred him to a government hospital where he died a few days later.

We felt death's sting, and like Jesus taught us to do, we wept.

Flovia recovered further, and within three months, she was able to be discharged to a children's home in our community.

* * *

Asking a guiding question about love—and exploring its answers—does not imply that either I or my team are saviors. It is much more about noticing one person's worth, recognizing the suffering of those who've been pushed to the margins. It's about being willing to accompany one another through both joy and pain, and to do so with vulnerability. It's believing that the way of Jesus is to love and be loved in tangible ways.

Unbeknownst to us, Flovia and Felix would be the first of hundreds, then thousands, who would come into our care. In the most profound ways, these beautiful babies would teach us about the mysteries of God. About a kind of love that is as big as it is wide. Compassion and a willingness to try led us to begin something as small as a mustard seed that grew over time into what has become the Living Room.

We didn't know it was coming. None of us do when we answer the call to love. We are simply invited to be willing to try.

* * *

Recently, I listened to my son Geoffrey's prayer before supper: "Help those who are hungry have food to eat. Help those who need peace to find it."

I'm not sure how he learned to pray like this, but it always moves me. Not long before, he prayed at bedtime, "Thank you, God, for choosing the weak things of the world" (see 1 Cor 1:27).

I didn't teach him this verse. It is simply within him, this child who has experienced loss and suffered more in his eight years than some have in a lifetime. And somehow, because the words come from him, there is more room for the truth of them to grow within me.

What if God also chooses the things that feel weak and unsure within you and me to accomplish what our self-confidence and certainty never could?

What if he chose the tired parts of me from hundreds of scary nights spent on a hospital sleeper chair? From the tears that come easier than I am comfortable with but also tell me I am still alive, that we somehow survived. From the hard unknowns that still lurk around many corners.

What if my personal experience of watching my children suffer to the point of death doesn't crush me but surprisingly makes space for more compassion to grow within me?

The courage that comes through vulnerability has a way of reshaping our priorities, how we see ourselves and those around us, making room for us to appreciate the things we truly hunger for: being seen, being told we have value and are worthy of love.

It's the brave love my team at the Living Room and I said yes to when we decided to try all those years ago with Flovia and Felix.

The same love tenderly calls from within, "Be kind to yourself," welcoming the fragile parts of me to be noticed and named.

It's the love that invites you and me, today and tomorrow and, again, the next day, to lean into the seemingly impossible situations that fill our lives, homes, and neighborhoods.

What if we all sang in chorus,
"Who is like me?"
without a hint of comparison or judgment.
Perhaps we'd know more of God
and have the eyes to see.
We are loved and worthy of it
as our sole identity.

Chapter Three

Honoring Life

A photograph from some ten years ago, pre-Titus and pre-motherhood, shows me standing beside a six-year-old boy named Evans, a guest at Kimbilio Hospice. Evans, an orphan who had suffered terribly in his short stint on this planet, had been referred to us from the HIV treatment center because he was malnourished and failing to thrive. His eyes already blind from complications related to HIV/AIDS, Evans arrived at the hospice so weak that he was unable to sit up or speak.

Medicine, food, and enough time allowed Evans to gain weight and increase in strength. When he began to learn how to navigate his way around the hospice with his new walking stick, he found his voice and began to speak and sing again.

"*Yaya*," one of Evans's first words, was an unfamiliar word to me, and yet he kept saying it whenever I was around. I asked Muthoni, another guest from the same tribe as Evans, "*Anasema nini?*" What is he saying?

She giggled as she translated, "Juli, he's calling you the maid."

"Oh!" Surprised and somehow delighted, we laughed together. The term of endearment, as I liked to think of it, stuck, and all the other verbal children at the hospice joined in and called me Yaya, too.

Even though Evans could no longer see with his eyes, he'd hold my face in both of his hands to discover more of who I was, smiling widely and calling me "Yaya." In those moments, I discovered more of who he was. Beyond his physical impairments and the labels so easily attached to him was a beautiful boy who brought joy to all of us.

I am convinced that, with the right opportunity, Evans could have been a brilliant musician. He loved to whistle and would throw his head back as he played the harmonica he discovered while in our care. Evans sang, too, but only one song—a popular Kenyan gospel song with lyrics that say, *Nani kama wewe?* Who is like you, in reference to God. Only, he never sang those words. He always sang, *Nani kama mimi?* Who is like me?

For a while, our team tried to correct Evans's lyrics, but he continued to sing over and again, *Nani kama mimi?* And I began to wonder the same thing. Evans was wonderfully made, and we were the privileged ones that got to honor his life and care for him in all his strength and vulnerability.

On the day seizures took over Evans's body and he died, our hearts broke wide open. It wasn't the story we wanted for him or for us. It wasn't the outcome we hoped for.

We grieved because we loved him, because we felt the void of Evans's presence, the absence of his beautiful voice filling our hallways.

* * *

"I'm trying to make sense out of senseless things, in senseless ways," I tell my counselor, Ben, who's on the other side of the world in LA.

"Isn't that what you do every day, Juli?"

I'm sitting outside of Kimbilio Hospice by myself, looking at a bright blue sky. We've survived our boys' transplants and now are trying to find our way through a global pandemic.

There's a plethora of green surrounding and calming me, shades that might even be specific to the village I call home. I hear birds singing, cows mooing, roosters crowing.

Instinctively, I breathe it all in along with the cool morning air and exhale loudly.

Ben pauses to allow room for silence before he continues. "Every day, Juli, you care for the sick and dying. You live amongst suffering and abject poverty. Every day, you are trying to make sense."

Tears run down my face as I process, yet again, the reality that living and loving involves holding the tension of the beautiful and the broken things within and around me.

I attempt to convey the relationship between my mind trying to understand situations outside of my control and my desire for justice and mercy and humility to prevail. For a broken world to be a little less broken. For broken bodies to find relief, to be made well. For broken hearts to know they are loved.

I could only nod as my nine-year-old Ella and I were recently walking and she said, "Mom, I believe God loves and protects us, and I also believe that sometimes bad things happen in this world."

I had been trying to comfort her, to minimize her fear, but she and I both knew what she said was true.

I go outside every day, to sit, to walk, to stand on solid ground. I need my senses to be alive, reminding me I still have desires. I may be disappointed, waiting, aching, longing, but seeing, hearing, smelling, tasting, touching somehow reminds me of the breath in my body and the presence of hope.

I can't make sense out of the senseless things, but outside, I can somehow quiet my soul and listen for the God who, above all things, I know to be loving and kind. Outside, I can pursue wholeness and resist despair.

* * *

In September 2017, when Ryan and Geoffrey needed bone marrow transplants at UCLA, friends who live in Los Angeles invited us to "just come, and we'll figure it out."

What Titus and I and these friends, the Herbert family, all thought this meant was that we'd come and stay in their home for a few weeks until their guest house was renovated. This alone was generous and kind of Baba Micah, Mama Micah, and their son, Micah, a high school senior at the time. But what it actually turned out to be was our family of six living in their home, with them, for 477 days. Fifteen months of cultural differences, language barriers, drastically different lived experiences, multiple losses, and chronic illness that accompanied us.

And all of this while we Boits were still learning to become a family.

I often said to Mama Micah, "I became a mom like two minutes ago and went from one child to however many we have." To say the least, we were complicated. Yet, 10,000 miles away from home, this family made space in their lives to welcome us.

After we returned to Kenya, we still felt held and loved by the Herberts. I'd often write to Mama Micah and share about the wonder of watching the boys learn to climb trees, even on the days when there were still reminders of the scars. Reminders like the fact that Geoffrey had had a stroke back when sickle cell disease still waged war in his body.

A remnant of the stroke, Geoffrey's spastic right foot makes balance and walking a tricky thing, requiring him to wear a brace. Since the transplants, we travel back to the US each year for follow-up medical appointments for the boys and get Geoffrey fitted for a new brace.

The challenge, or one of the many, is finding a shoe to fit over the brace. Since he wears the brace on only one foot, two different sizes are needed. Certain companies make extra wide shoes and sell single shoes to accommodate special needs. But the bulkiness of Geoffrey's brace makes it nearly impossible to find any shoe that fits. And yet we keep trying.

Geoffrey chooses the colors and patterns for each new brace—we've had Spiderman, dinosaurs, and Scooby-doo. Every time we go for the casting and fitting of a new one, he gets excited, like it will be a magic fix and he'll be able to run freely with his siblings and friends.

So far, it hasn't worked out that way.

One day, Geoffrey, Mama Micah, and I returned to the orthotic shop to pick up his new brace. I don't know why, but I asked him a ridiculous question: "What kind of shoes do you want to wear over your new dinosaur brace?"

With light in his eyes, Geoffrey said, "I'd like rainbow shoes."

Trying to fix my misstep, I quickly replied, "Geoffrey, we will do our best to find rainbow shoes, but mostly we need to find anything that can work with your brace."

A few hours later, with a tower of twenty-three boxes of shoes sitting beside him, Geoffrey looked past Mama

Micah's shoulder to the wall display. "Look!" he said. "Rainbow shoes!"

I turned around and saw red, yellow, green, and blue with a Nike swoosh across the side of a white sneaker. Geoffrey looked at Mama Micah and me, two unsuspecting mothers who have the greatest privilege in all the world to love this little boy, and said, "I get to have rainbow shoes. God keeps his promises, you know?"

Only, he didn't say it like it was a question for him, but rather for me. In the shoe department at Nordstrom, that day, I was unexpectedly being invited to choose, once more, to trust the kindness and mystery of the God who had seen and honored my little boy's dreams for rainbow shoes, a request I had tried to reign in as too extravagant. Couldn't God also see and hear the cry of my heart, for healing and wholeness for my family and me, in the aftermath of so much pain?

Needless to say, we got two pairs of different-sized rainbow Nike shoes that day, though we had to order them from Chicago since no store in LA had them in stock. Every time I see these shoes, I smile and remember: in a world that so often doesn't make sense, where hard things happen, God keeps his promises.

* * *

Five years after moving to Kenya, the dream of building a hospice home of sorts rose stronger within me every day. Our small team had lovingly cared for Flovia and Felix and felt the growing need within our community.

I was home in LA, and over a Quiznos sandwich, I told my brother and a dear friend, Jacob, about the dream growing within me to build a hospice. I imagined it would become a place where people who were sick and dying could be welcomed to come as they are and be treated with compassion and dignity.

I was unsure of next steps and asked if they would pray for me.

A month or two later, Jacob wrote, "Juli, I can't get the idea of the home for the dying out of my head. Every time I talk to God about it, I refer to it as the Living Room."

A lump formed in my throat, and tears filled my eyes at the phrase. *Living Room.* On so many levels, it captured what I hoped it might become.

Fast forward about a year, and my team and I were registering a non-profit organization and building a 24-bed hospice. At the heart of our work would be this vision:

"Living Room is to be a community of compassion that honors life and offers hope."

These words would be written into the walkway on each end of the ramp at Living Room's Kimbilio Hospice: "Honouring Life and Offering Hope."

At Living Room, rather than calling a person who comes into the hospice a patient, we refer to them as *mgeni,* a guest. We wanted each man, woman, or child to know that they were loved and welcomed.

One morning, as I was greeting the guests at Kimbilio Hospice, one of them—a man whose name and story I didn't yet know—sat on the front veranda. He held my hand and spoke unexpected words that felt like a blessing of sorts: *"Asante kwa kuniona."* Thank you for seeing me.

I nodded and allowed his words to slip into my heart as a clarion of what we are all called to do. To see in such a way as to love. To affirm one another's value and worth by the way we pay attention.

Sunita Puri, a palliative care physician, wrote, "I have learned to look when I want to look away. I have chosen to stay when I'd prefer to run out of the room and cry. The prelude to compassion is the willingness to see."[6]

6 Sunita Puri, *We Must Learn to Look at Grief, Even When We Want to Run Away,* New York Times (February 23, 2022).

Each day, there are opportunities aplenty, in whatever neighborhood you and I might find ourselves, to see the person in front of us, allowing the lines of brokenness and beauty to blur together. In this world, we will experience untellable grief and loss, but we can also experience blessing and love.

* * *

My life and work in Kenya have been shaped immensely by a mentor whose great courage and compassion I was privileged not only to witness, but also invited to participate in. It is an honor I will always be grateful for.

On an early Friday morning in January of 2005, three months after I moved to Kenya, I brought a man dying of complications related to HIV/AIDS to a one-room clinic in Turbo, ten miles away from where I lived. A tall, seventy-year-old white doctor with a North Carolina accent stood in the doorway holding a patient file in hand.

"Hello, I'm Joe," he said, his voice and temperament radiating kindness. "What are you doing here in the middle of nowhere?"

"Hello, I'm Juli." I told him that I lived in a nearby village and was tired of watching people die of a treatable disease, but I didn't have access to testing or medications for HIV.

Joe invited me into a room filled with test kits and antiretrovirals that only minutes before had felt a world away. Right there before us, they sat making what felt utterly impossible a whole lot less so.

Something shifted in every fiber of my being.

I learned, though not from Joe, that he was a renowned professor of medicine from Indiana University, nominated multiple times for the Nobel Peace Prize. Humble and wholeheartedly committed to the care of his patients, Joe spent his retirement years building one of the largest and most successful HIV treatment programs in the world.

Each Friday morning for nearly a decade, I sat beside him in a treatment room at the HIV clinic in Turbo as a line of people with untellable suffering filled the corridor, waiting for their turn to see the doctor. They were sicker than anything I'd ever seen or imagined. Each story resembled the one from before—extraordinary suffering, one after another.

Joe carried a blue medical bag and the same stethoscope he'd been using for fifty years. It had listened to the hearts of men, women, and children all over the world. He'd pay attention to each person in front of us as if they were his family member and would frequently say with perfect clarity, "She is my mother. He is my son. As long as I remember *that*, everything else makes sense."

Five years into my friendship with Joe, I shared with him my idea of building a hospice. He asked me challenging, important questions and told me that he believed in me and would support me in whatever ways he could, often reminding me that we can't wait until something is perfect to begin. "We necessarily plan, of course," he'd say, "but the key lesson seems to be to begin."

And so, we began.

* * *

Years later, during the height of the COVID-19 crisis, I listened to a beautiful podcast about what it was like to be a nurse in the middle of the pandemic. The guest said that at the core of nursing was the ability to love a stranger.

I would add that there's still another level. Like Joe so lovingly taught me and demonstrated in practical ways: *There is a deeper level still—where we begin to recognize that there is no such thing as a stranger.*

In Kenya, instead of using the word *period* to refer to the end of a sentence, we refer to a *full stop*. I'd like to propose that at the core of nursing is the ability to love. Full stop. No other qualifiers. It's not about being perfect or a superhero.

In the same way, the core of being a human being and a neighbor is in our love. Full stop.

What might it look like for us to notice and value the image of God uniquely imprinted on each one of us? How might it affect the way you and I go through our days?

Perhaps, simply, though not to be confused with ease, we would grow, day by day, in the ways of compassion, honoring the lives of our patients, our neighbors, and ourselves.

Making room for what is.
For what is yet to be.
For welcomes and boundaries.
For healing and wholeness.
For the wounded and weary
parts of you and me.
For questions like:
What if? And why not?
Space for love and possibility.

Chapter Four

Making Room

After supper, Ella sits in my lap to read a story. At seven, she's no longer the wiggly toddler with an unlimited energy reserve. Her curiosity feels as tall as she has become. Like me, she's trying to make sense of the world and who she is within it.

She explores every nook and cranny, every grasshopper, butterfly, and bird. She speaks Swahili as she plays with her friends. With bare feet, she climbs the smooth, red-brown bark of the *mapera* tree and then sits within it to eat unripe guava while observing all the happenings of village life around her.

Ella runs an animal hospital for her stuffed animals, which is a step up from the one she led for live bees during our transplant season in Los Angeles—that is, until she came across "a mean one." During COVID times, Ella often delayed starting school in the morning as she put her stuffed lemur on a ventilator.

The book we read together tonight she can read by herself. But I am grateful she still crawls on my lap and lets me read it with her. At first glance, she says the little girl on the cover looks just like her—"blond" skinned, as she calls her brown skin, with fluffy hair.

We read the exquisite words of Jacqueline Woodson: "So like the people who came before us, we lifted our arms even higher, closed our eyes even tighter, breathed in even deeper, and flew the way we'd always known how to... free as our own beautiful and brilliant minds."[7]

Later in the story, Woodson resolved, "Sometimes the first step toward change is closing our eyes, taking a breath, and imagining a different way."

Often, when I watch a yellow and black weaverbird carrying a long blade of grass to create a nest, making a shelter for its babies to come, I think about the "nests" I've tried to make for my babies, here in Kenya, and the one woven for us in Los Angeles by Baba and Mama Micah.

More than anything, I want to protect my children, keep them safe from all that could and will inevitably

---

7 Jacqueline Woodson, *The Year We Learned to Fly* (New York: Nancy Paulsen Books, 2022), location 17, Kindle edition.

hurt them. But what does it mean for them, and for me as their mother, to imagine a different way? A way that is bigger and roomier for them to grow and flourish, allowing for the complexity of their stories, the losses as well as the miracles?

* * *

I lie under the canopy of my mosquito net, tired but awake. Who knows exactly why I choose to click on a link at 3 a.m. to take an IQ test. It clearly doesn't help my insomnia or, honestly, anything at all.

Nonetheless, somewhere around question thirteen, I am asked: "True or False, if you remove seven letters from the word *motherhood*, the letters for the word *home* will remain."

Before I can click "false," seeing that it's six instead of seven, I pause, both surprised and delighted that the letters making up the word *home* live in both mother and motherhood. And I wonder if, somehow, in the depths of us all, they are one and the same.

Everyone's home of origin is within their mother's body. I remember the overwhelming, instinctual desire I had when I was pregnant with Ella to remake our house to welcome her, this baby girl growing within my womb.

The one who would stretch me in ways that can never be undone.

A poem by John O'Donohue, which lent me the name of my first book, *From Beyond the Skies*, beautifully speaks to this:

Nothing could have prepared

Your heart to open like this.

From beyond the skies and the stars

This echo arrived inside you.

And started to pulse with life,

Each beat a tiny act of growth,

Traversing all our ancient shapes

On its way home to itself.

Once it began, you were no longer your own.[8]

Two and a half years later, I felt a similar invitation, only it didn't come from a baby growing within me. Instead, it was a tiny newborn whose mother died on the same day as his birth. It unexpectedly opened every crevice of my heart to make space for him.

---

8 John O'Donohue, *To Bless the Space Between Us: A Book of Blessings* (New York: Doubleday, 2008), 56.

Ryan wasn't "mine" to mother, but I wanted so badly for him to survive, to be protected. And so, Titus, Ella, and I made room, even if temporarily, to welcome him into our home.

Some nineteen months later, the instinct arose again, fierce as it was tender. I needed to build another nest, this time in a hospital room where our little boy would undergo a daunting bone marrow transplant.

I folded stacks of cozy, toddler-sized pajamas and beanies to warm his soon-to-be bald head and placed them in a blue duffle bag. I would decorate the space, wanting him and everyone else who entered it to know just how loved he was, that he was more than a medical condition or bed number.

And, four months later, I'd do it again to some degree—exhausted, hesitant, and spent beyond anything I'd ever known—when it was Geoffrey's turn for a transplant. My resistance, this time, was that I didn't know if it would be enough to protect him. I didn't want to face the chance that we could lose him as we so nearly did with Ryan.

Now, on the other side of those harrowing 481 days in LA, I wondered what would be required of me to rebuild our home in Kenya and show up for my family.

I wondered whether I had the strength to do what love asked of me—yet again.

How could I, piece by piece, put a nest together to protect and nurture my babies? To allow room for my kids and family to navigate through the tender, uncharted journey of our wounds turning into scars. Isn't this what every mother does after every trauma, every scare, big or small, that takes her to the end of herself?

Hillary McBride writes about our ability to look back and mourn a traumatic experience when we're on the other side of it. "We may anticipate relief, and while that may come, when we realize the grief comes from the sense that we are no longer in danger, we can trust the grief and the goodness in it: it is the witnessing we deserved all along. Grieving is part of healing."[9]

Grieving is part of healing, and I had many losses to notice and name. Time and space—and grace—were required for us all to be reoriented to a new home and culture. To languages my littlest ones once knew by heart but no longer could remember. Even to the sound of rain on our tin roof.

We had to notice and remember how and why Sharon, Alice, Geoffrey, and Ryan came to be a part of

---

9 Hillary McBride, "Something Happens When We Have Been Through a Trauma," Instagram photo, January 20, 2023, https://bit.ly/3pyIBV2.

our family in the first place, that their loss and grief had become ours, too.

We now felt the wonder of having the "healing" we had so desperately longed for, in addition to feeling the remnants of all it cost to get us to this point. For this step, "home" and "mothering" required me to make room within my nest, within my soul, for the messiness and complexity of grief as a part of our family's path toward healing—and this path required much more than removing six letters.

* * *

One late Sunday morning, weeks after returning to Kenya from the boys' transplants, I looked across the garden at Kimbilio to see a woman standing in the shade of a vibrant bougainvillea. Her thirty-year-old son, barely conscious, reclined in a wheelchair beside her. Brain cancer was doing its best to take his life.

This mama and her son were surrounded by singing as other patients and staff gathered for an impromptu service in the garden. They sang songs of praise and gave accounts of how God was with them, giving them hope.

In a tender moment, I looked over to see this mama lean down and rest her face against her son's. While he was a grown man, he was still her child. This look of love felt so familiar to me—she wanted to take his place.

I looked at her and saw a mother whose son was fearfully and wonderfully made from the depths beneath her heart. Before he ever filled her arms, he knew her from the inside. And now, it neared the time for him to leave, to go without her. The anguish and unrelenting grief were all held in a moment as she rested her face against his, waiting for him to die.

Not long before, I had sat in on a series of interviews to hire the new staff for Living Room's hospital in Eldoret. We received and read 8,000 applications for sixty positions. In one of the interviews for a chaplain position, I went off-script and asked, "If a child has just passed away and the grieving mother asks you, 'Where is my child now?' what would you tell her?"

I understood it may be a complicated question for some, but it felt very important to me. I asked on behalf of all the grieving parents who might seek refuge in our care. But even as I asked the question, I knew, in part, I was also asking it for me, as I still carried the tenderness and awareness of how close we came to losing our son, Ryan.

I don't remember the response he gave. I wasn't searching for a "right answer," but rather the compassion with which the answer might be given. For all the mamas to come, I needed to know Living Room would be loving and gentle with their broken hearts.

* * *

What makes room for us to reimagine our lives, families, churches, and neighborhoods as God dreams them to be? *A different sort of way* that involves justice and mercy, moving beyond our thoughts and words and spilling over into the actions of our lives.

On any given day, Kimbilio Hospice has extraordinary cases come our way. People show up on the back of a *pikipiki*, motorbike taxi, looking for help and not sure where to go. Their stories and struggles are, at times, almost unfathomable.

Once, an elderly gentleman named Arap Sang came into our doors after his fingers and toes started to self-amputate. It was progressing, and he didn't have an official diagnosis, but he had been told that Kimbilio was a place of prayer. So he came.

When he arrived, I immediately called my friend, Dr. Joe, and shared about his case and asked him for help. "What do you advise?"

"Well, Juli," Dr. Joe replied, "he most likely has some sort of vasculitis and needs either the Mayo Clinic or

Living Room. Nothing in the middle will do. So, it looks like he's in the right place. Does he have pain?"

"No pain. He's comfortable," I said.

"How do these people always end up with you at Living Room?"

"You tell me."

Over the next few days, Joe's question lingered with me: *How do these people always end up at Living Room?*

The answer, I am sure, is multi-layered. But of this, I am convinced: the "hopeless ones" from far and wide that keep finding their way to Kimbilio Hospice matter to God. Their suffering matters to us, and we want to keep making room for them to be welcomed at Living Room. A place where the most vulnerable—the hungry, the lonely, the disabled, the dying—come and are treated with dignity.

They come, and we look into their eyes and listen to their stories, even when they sometimes cannot speak. We bind wounds, believing that everything done with love is holy to God.

When we gather as guests and staff of Living Room, everyone brings their own lived experience and story. As we come together, we often sing. Sometimes planned, other times impromptu.

The songs are most often hymns or gospel songs sung in Swahili or another tribal language. They seem to include both individual reflection and communal pronouncement.

Together, we say "thank you" to God or cry out in longing for the day when sorrow, pain, and death will be no more. We remind ourselves that God sees and knows and loves all of us.

* * *

I've had moments to sit alongside a Kimbilio Hospice guest named Janet, a woman who speaks no words but sings throughout the day and night. Her repertoire consists of exactly two songs: a Swahili hymn that says, "I am so glad that Jesus loves me," and a Luhya song talking of the cross.

She hits the arm of her chair in rhythm as if she is beating a drum and sings, "Hallelujah." I mostly listen, absorbing the weight of the words she sings. Sometimes, I join in and sing hallelujah, too.

At Kimbilio, we make room for those who are weary and wounded. At times, that has included me. In days and seasons filled with doubt and unanswerable questions, with tears of disappointment and loss, I've found the comfort of a community well practiced in weeping with those who weep.

Amid the brokenness, though, a song is quietly hummed, or sometimes shouted, through the hallways—a song of a love greater than darkness. A love which is tender, personal, and kind. A love stronger than death.

There's a tradition in Kenya called *harambee*, meaning "all pull together." It's about coming together as a community to stand with one another as everyone is able, in both good and hard times.

I see *harambee* being practiced in Living Room, where we "all pull together," making room for one another and the space for both sorrow and joy to sit side by side. I sit within it, too, in my humanity. I sit as a nurse and advocate for our patients, as well as a mama trying to navigate my children's needs, my own needs.

Steve Reifenberg writes, "Accompaniment flips the impulse of 'How do we help them?' into an assertion—'We're in this together.' We need to walk together and learn together, and maybe, together, we can envision and create better, more equitable tomorrows, both for the big issues 'over there' and also in our daily lives, loving our neighbors—that is, everyone—as we love ourselves."[10]

As we pull together, we remind one another that we aren't alone. Like the words I read in the storybook with Ella, we lift our arms higher, close our eyes tighter, breathe in deeper, and make room for each other, for what is, and for what may come.

---

10 Steve Reifenberg, *In the Company of the Poor: Conversations with Dr. Paul Farmer and Gustavo Gutierrez* (Maryknoll: Orbis Books, 2013), 196.

Will you be my neighbor?

And will I be yours?

Crossing the street—

to say hello, karibu, welcome.

I need help, or how can I help?

To borrow a cup of sugar,

to share a flask of chai,

to sit quietly beside in times of grief,

to sing and dance, to celebrate.

My loss is yours.

Yours is mine.

Showing up—

the cost and the reward of love.

Chapter Five

Being A Neighbor

My morning commute to Kimbilio Hospice involves a mile and a half walk through our village, a neighborhood I've walked through for the past nineteen years. When I moved to Kenya in 2004, I thought I was coming for a year, maybe two, to be a part of a team doing HIV work in the community. But the more I listened and learned and dove deep into relationships with my patients and neighbors, the more I wanted to stay.

Who I was then compared to who I am now is likely connected to the number of miles I've walked along this road. What do I see now compared to what I noticed then? What feels the same and what has changed within and around me?

When I first visited Kenya in the summer of 2000 as a nursing student on a short-term trip, I met David Tarus.

David is a community leader of our village, a friend, and now an executive director at Living Room.

As an act of hospitality, he generously gave me and the others on our team Kalenjin names. It was an honor, unexpected, undeserved, and deeply meaningful. A name by which I would be known. A name that was easy for my neighbors to remember and pronounce. A name that powerfully communicated to me and them that I was a welcomed member of this community.

Like many African communities, the Kalenjin tribe names their children based on the events surrounding the birth. They consider the season, place of birth, weather, mom's situation at birth, or time of day.

David gave me the name *Jepkios*, meaning I was born prematurely, before my time. On the day I came into the world, I was a five-pound baby, born three weeks early. As my mom's labor pains began, she told my dad, "The baby is coming, and I'm not ready!" Twenty-one years later, on the other side of the world, I was given a name related to my prematurity.

David introduced me and other visitors to the community by our Kalenjin names. "*Yeye, sio mzungu. Anaitwa* Jepkios." Don't call her "white person" (or more literally, "wanderer"). Her name is Jepkios. He'd go on to say, "*Pokea huyu.*" Receive her.

Until I married Titus, some eight years after arriving in Kenya, people in the area knew me as Jepkios. As I'd walk from house to house doing home visits, or to the hospice after it was built, people greeted me along the way as they did all their neighbors.

The mama selling bananas and green oranges at a small kiosk on the side of the road called out, "*Chamgei* Jepkios." Hello!

"*Chamgei*," I'd reply.

Or Peter, a cobbler, whose arms were strong from pushing himself long distances throughout the village in his blue wheelchair to repair shoes. Stopping beside a hedge of lantana, pink and yellow flowers blooming among green leaves, he'd smile and say, "*Chamgei* Jepkios."

"*Chamgei*."

For years, a man I called *Agui,* grandfather, sat in the center of the village, grand and well-aged as the mango tree he sat beside. He carried a wooden walking stick always in his hand, while cows and sheep, a handful of chickens, grazed close by. Agui loved to greet me as I walked past him on many a day.

I'm certain it wasn't just me, but he always made me feel special. "Jepkios?" he'd ask each time.

"*Wei*," I'd nod.

"*Ochamagei*." Hello!

"*Chamaagei*, Agui."

After the shaking of hands and the back and forth of greetings, Agui would continue to speak in Kalenjin, with more vocabulary and depth than I understood. Rightfully, he insisted upon my learning. When he finished lecturing me, he'd throw his head back and laugh, delighted that we had met.

Agui didn't mince words. If I ever failed to stop and greet him because I was late or in a hurry, he'd also let me know that I needed to pause, to remember that people and relationships are more important than time and schedules. By saying hello, we repeatedly honored each other's worth. Agui was a good friend and teacher.

I walked the road by myself many a day but always loved the times when my dearest friend, Allison—David's wife—joined me. We'd process the lives we lived so far away from our original homes, talking about the home visit we'd just come from, or how we needed to take deworming medication to the local primary school.

Allison and I shared the desire to be humble learners within a culture outside of our own. We asked many questions of each other, laughing and crying our way through, walking together under the bright, warm sun.

Before electricity came to the village, I walked the roads that filled this quiet village with exquisite beauty, complex challenges, and generous hospitality. I walked them before there was access to clean water, piped to taps, then collected and carried in jerry cans. Before *pikipikis* drove up and down the dirt road, precariously ferrying more people and goods than seemed possible. Before I was married or a mother, when I was more certain of so many things.

I came to understand this place and its people better with time, through proximity. I learned to appreciate simplicity that should not be confused with ease. I struggled to make sense of needless suffering as a result of abject poverty and treatable diseases. I sang and danced at weddings to celebrate love. I visited mamas in their homes to say, *"Pongezi,"* congratulations, after their baby was born. I listened to prayers asking God for literal daily bread.

When I married Titus, my name changed from Jepkios to *Nebo Arap Boit*, Mrs. Boit.

A year later, in 2013, my Kalenjin name shifted to *Bot Jerop*, Mama Jerop. Born on a rainy day, my brown-eyed wonder of a girl gave me a new name. It shifted my identity and role in the world, within this community.

My name, along with so many other things, has changed as I've continued to walk along this same path.

I've watched children whose mothers I assisted during childbirth grow from a newborn baby, overdressed in a winter jacket and woolen hat, to preschoolers and school-aged children, walking the same path as me in their school uniforms. Some have gone to high school and, against all sorts of odds, finished. Some look for work, others farm or search for the chance to go to college.

Day after day, year upon year, a rainbow of colors from hand-washed clothes drying on their lines have greeted me along with a generation of little boys and girls who offered to teach me to run when they were little but have now grown up.

A new set of children, including my own, are on the road now, greeting me by name, wooing me with their bright smiles and magical play.

These years of walking have taught me that motherhood—when lived in community—extends beyond our own children. Within this village, each little one is seen as the joy and responsibility of all. They are daily reminders of beauty and brokenness, of curiosity and the possibility of what it might look like to love and be loved within a neighborhood. Yesterday, today, and, God willing, in the years to come.

* * *

"Mom, there is something special about living in Kenya," Ella said a few months ago, as we walked near the stream in the evening light. We had just passed children happily harvesting *kumbe kumbe*, termites, from the hill. They placed one termite after another in their plastic bags to take home and fry as a tasty treat. This place has always been home for Ella.

"What makes it so special for you?"

She thought for just a moment. "The sky and our neighbors."

"Yes, it's very special, Ella."

She later asked me about one of her friends who comes over to play and is often hungry and doesn't have shoes. "Mom, what if I don't want to just notice? I want to help."

The depth of her sincerity moved me.

"Ella, I think you help."

"Yeah. Me, too," she said. The next afternoon she started sorting through which shoes she would share.

* * *

One night, long before I had my own children, I shared a simple meal with David, Allison, and their family by the light of a kerosene lantern. It was early in my time in Kenya, and we were discussing the events of the day. David became quiet for a few moments, and then his distinct voice choked up as he asked me, "Do you hear the cries of the poor?"

David pays attention to those who struggle in their daily lives—to have enough food to eat, to afford medical care, to pay school fees for their children's education, to access clean drinking water.

He listens, but he also knows that God hears their cries and cares how we notice and respond.

David's question felt like a sacred invitation to share some of the weight of the listening, of the paying attention. Of the aching and the hoping for what has not yet come. Of the commitment to justice and mercy, believing these are the antithesis of poverty.

Jesus was born into a community and lived among neighbors. When he grew up and met Andrew and John, who would become his followers and friends, they once asked Jesus where he lived. He replied, "Come along and see for yourself" (see John 1:35–39).

In Kipkaren, we don't have to schedule dinners or play dates to get together. When we stop by a neighbor's home, it's perceived as a blessing.

"*Hodi,*" we say. I'm here.

"*Karibu.*" Welcome, feel at home, is always the response.

When Jesus welcomed Andrew and John into where he was staying, I imagine him saying in Swahili, "*Karibu.*"

In Kenyan culture, if you wave your hand by folding your fingers up and down, it isn't a greeting of "hello." It's a signal, meaning *kuja,* come. I see Jesus, in this story, waving to his new friends, saying, "*Kuja,*" come and see. Have a cup of chai. Let's spend time together.

John repeatedly writes of how his identity was reshaped in the three years he spent alongside Jesus, how he came to understand and experience that he was loved. This is what living in a loving community can do for all of us. And this is what I often experience daily, living among my neighbors in Kenya.

* * *

A few months after I moved to Kenya in 2005, I met a woman from our village named Betty. She showed up on a hot Saturday afternoon at an HIV-awareness training we were conducting.

Betty sat in the back of the room. At the end of the session, she volunteered to share her story with the group.

"A few months ago," Betty shared in Swahili, "I was very sick and had given up hope. Everyone was afraid of me, afraid of my sickness. They no longer wanted to greet me."

You could hear a pin drop. With a gentle confidence, Betty continued. "One night, I was sleeping alone in our kitchen, so weak and tired of always being sick. I looked up and could see the stars through the patches where the grass was missing on the roof. I cried out to a God I didn't really know, and I asked Him to either take my life so I could rest or restore me so that I could live for Him."

She wasn't afraid to look people in the eye. "A few days later, a friend advised me to go for HIV testing. The test takes only a few minutes—if it shows one line, it means you're negative. Two lines, positive. Mine showed two."

It was the first time I'd ever heard anyone in Kenya publicly announce that they were HIV positive. Here and there, people shifted in their seats, but Betty kept going.

"Everyone should go for testing. It's important to know your status. I have been taking the medicine for HIV and feel stronger than I have in a long time. It seems God is giving me back my life, and I am learning to live it for Him."

Betty sat down, the room quiet.

It was the first of a thousand steps toward breaking down the stigma plaguing HIV/AIDS at the time. Our team listened to Betty's story that day and embraced her, and she quickly became a part of our outreach team. She was trained to be an HIV counselor and tester, and she would do so, sharing her story, in the community and in awareness campaigns.

Once, while standing beside her on the veranda of my little round house, I asked her, "Why are you willing to share your story so openly? I know it is costly to you. Why do you do it?"

Betty looked me in the eyes as if I should have already understood. With the same authority she always seemed to speak, she said, "We all have talents, Juli. Some can sing or preach. I have HIV. One day when I stand before

God and he asks, 'What did you do with your talent?' I will tell him."

All I could do was nod in amazement.

Months later, we sat in her house as she crocheted a red and yellow blanket. The light from the open door frame shone on her face as she sat next to a greyish-brown wall of earthen clay. Betty looked me in the eyes and leaned forward, as if to tell me a secret. She smiled and whispered, "I think I am God's favorite."

Tears still fill my eyes when I remember the way she said it, the way she knew she was loved. All I could muster was, "Yes Betty, you most definitely are."

It's been over a decade since Betty left us to go and be with God. I often hear her voice in my head and like to think she's leading the ever-growing Living Room choir, singing praises to the God of love.

* * *

It's a remarkable thing to stay in the same neighborhood for so many years and to walk a well-acquainted path. I needed to leave it behind for 481 days, but I returned. To feel the ground once more beneath my feet. To feel gratitude for a mentor and friend who kindly welcomed me, giving me a name to help me belong. To feel grateful for his generous, although undeserved, instruction to the community: *"Pokea huyu."* Receive her. To walk past where Betty used to live, and to remember the beautiful things we shared. To remember the love she understood in ways I long to experience.

When I notice a colorful barbet in a fig tree, with a red bar across its wing, singing a raspy song, I am reminded to slow down, to listen longer. I'm thrilled by its beauty, and Jesus's words come to me: "If I take care of the birds, I will take care of you" (see Matt. 6:26–34).

This message of Jesus keeps drawing me outside on so many mornings to look for birds. To listen to the choir of their singing. To be reminded that being a neighbor involves noticing, helping, and being helped when it's needed. To recognize that loving-kindness and new mercies are available again today.

I'm still learning—
nothing disarms
our defenses, our pretenses
as being welcomed,
received as we are.

Nothing expands
our hearts, our homes
as making room.

We don't need fancy houses or perfect lives.
We need each other.

Chapter Six

Hospitality

There is a wooden sign nailed to the front door of our home that says, *"Karibu."* Welcome. The same word, hand-painted in vibrant colors on a cloth, hung on a closet door at Mama Micah's. In that room, two twin beds with bright sheets and colorful quilts, as well as another cozy nest constructed with a mattress on the floor in the corner, welcomed Sharon, Ella, and Geoffrey for fifteen months.

The cloth sign was waiting for us on the day we arrived, and it remained there each day until we left and carried it back to Kenya.

Karibu was at the heart of Mama Micah's words when she wrote to invite us to come. "The guest house conversion is small, but I think with some adjustment it could work. So, you are very welcome, if that proves to be what you need. I wish you could hear how eager people are to walk with you all through this. Your bold steps make everyone bold."

After we completed the treatment and left LA to come back as a family to Kenya, it was my turn again to be the non-citizen, a visitor in a foreign land. And in true Kenyan hospitality, the immigration agent stamped our passports, adding, *"Karibuni nyumbani."*[11] Welcome home.

On that same January day, when we drove into our village after 481 days away, the community gathered outside our home to collectively sing, dance, shout, and say, *"Karibuni nyumbani."*

We were paraded toward our gate, hugging each person along the way. Among the crowd were friends like Kibet and Mama Jesang, who looked me in the eyes and held my hand. *"Karibu,* Mama Ella."

* * *

Nearly three years earlier, when we welcomed Ryan into our home as a newborn baby, there wasn't a system or timeline guiding our steps or decisions. We wanted him to be safe and to have a chance to survive and grow.

About a month in, Titus nonchalantly announced one night as I changed Ryan's diaper by the light of a

---

11 *Karibuni Nyumbani* is used to say "welcome home" to more than one person.

flashlight, "He doesn't need to go anywhere." I shared this sentiment, which eventually led us into the process of adoption.

From the day we met Ryan, the Living Room team implemented layers of support for his seven brothers and sisters, but they lived outside the walls of our home. Slowly, those clear divisions blurred.

Titus and I began having more conversations about a bigger picture, one that included all of Ryan's siblings. It wasn't particularly well thought out, but at breakfast one morning, Titus casually said, "I don't want Ryan to grow up and ask why we didn't help his brothers and sisters."

We didn't try to clarify what this might mean in the moment. We just knew, somehow, the love we held for Ryan would guide our family.

The complexity and cruelty of sickle cell disease added unexpected and unpredictable challenges. When Ryan was just over a year old, Geoffrey and Alice both had a sickle cell crisis, requiring them to be admitted to a hospital in Eldoret. After ten days of treatment, Alice was ready for discharge. Geoffrey would follow some weeks later.

But where would they go to recover? We decided, for the time being, our home was the best option. Titus held Alice's hand and led her down the stairs from the pediatric ward to the car.

It is strange to think back on these "you are welcome" sort of moments that have transformed the shape of our family, as well as the shape of my heart. I didn't realize these were before-and-after markers, permanent shifts where our home was making room, not for guests, but for additional members.

We simply took one step at a time. This was the next step, both loving and right.

* * *

The words *hospice*, *hotel*, and *hospital* all stem from the same word, meaning both "guest" and "host." Historically, the heart of these words relates to welcoming weary travelers and the sick.

Kenyan culture is marked by rich hospitality, valued and practiced in community, within homes, and within the hotel industry. When we started Living Room, we believed it was both important and doable to translate the value of hospitality into Kimbilio Hospice.

We asked many questions of ourselves: What would it look like to be hospitable in our patient care? How could this rich, welcoming spirit be included in the processes of running a hospice? In the ways we communicate? How do we break down barriers not just for patients to get to Living Room, but also to receive care? How could we create a kind and welcoming environment?

Henri Nouwen, beloved spiritual writer, whose words have deeply impacted my life, once wrote, "Hospitality means primarily the creation of a free space where the stranger can enter and become a friend instead of an enemy. Hospitality is not to change people but to offer them space where change can take place… Hospitality is not a subtle invitation to adore the lifestyle of the host, but the gift of a chance for the guest to find his own."[12]

We knew it didn't cost more to be kind or to listen well. We wanted to be intentional about treating people with honor and respect, both toward our patients and our care team. Life-limiting sickness and poverty can cause great fragility in those who suffer from both.

Most of the patients coming to us were referred from the government hospital where they had shared a single bed with another patient—one person's head at each end of the bed. We wanted to reduce the anxiety and fear, the suffering, that hospitals create.

---

12 Henri Nouwen, "Hospitality," *Henri Nouwen Society,* February 18, 2021, https://bit.ly/3NC3O8C.

* * *

For the two decades I've lived in Kenya, David Tarus has always led with a strong emphasis on hospitality. He says, "There are many things we don't have to give, but we can sing, dance, and make people feel welcome."

When a visitor comes to Kimbilio from within Kenya or beyond, our staff and guests gather on the front veranda to welcome them. The chaplain plays his guitar and leads the singing in a call-and-response style, singing about hugs and love. The choir echoes back while clapping their hands.

Upon arriving, visitors are ushered down the ramp toward the sound of singing. If it is their first visit, they often don't understand what's going on, that the singing is for them.

As they step over the words on the walkway that talk about life and hope, they see colorful pink and white ribbons tied across two posts at the end. It is like a threshold, separating the singing hosts who welcome from those being received. One of the visitors will be called by name and asked to come forward and cut the ribbon, symbolizing that now there is no longer separation. A guest from the hospice, often sitting in a wheelchair, waits to extend scissors for this ceremonial ribbon cutting.

To be received with intention and honor is disarming, and it often evokes deep emotion in the visitors. Each one is given a small bouquet of roses as the singing continues, and then they are led around the circle of Living Room staff and guests to shake hands with each of them.

Upon completing the greeting, David leads introductions so that people are known by name. From there, for those who are available and able, we walk to the field next to Kimbilio, and the visitors plant a tree.

The hole for the sapling is already dug, and a towel is laid down for the visitors to kneel and place the tree into the ground. All the while, a team from Kimbilio accompanies the process with singing. They hand the visitors a shovel to scoop dirt into the hole and a watering can to soak the tree.

We always close by praying for the tree to grow, to one day bear fruit. Then, David explains that, long after the visitors leave, their sapling will remain as their "embassy," growing to provide shade to the people at Kimbilio.

Planting a tree is a visitor's long-term investment, serving as a marker and remembrance of the gift of their coming. A metal sign will be placed beside the tree, labeling its type, the visitor's name, and the date it was planted.

The tradition of welcoming visitors into the community started long before Living Room existed, but the aspect of planting trees started organically when Living Room began. I don't remember any conversations about it, we just started doing it. Somehow, it stuck.

Like so many things done in our work, planting trees feels like an offering of hope. It takes years for the tree to grow, for it to bear fruit, but it is an investment requiring foresight and patience. It requires an imagination involving both action today and consideration for years to come, for generations to follow.

If you walk around Kimbilio Hospice grounds today, you will find over eight hundred trees with names and dates attached. The trees are of varying heights and sizes, and they span over a decade of planting.

What started small has grown into a large orchard across our twenty-two-acre campus. Visitors are viewed as a blessing in Kenyan culture. Walking around Kimbilio's grounds, seeing all of these living reminders of visitors through the years, you can see evidence that we are, indeed, blessed.

* * *

When we started Kimbilio Hospice in 2009, we dug a borehole, a 450-foot well on the land. Remarkably, we received an abundance of water, up to five thousand liters an hour. We attached a solar-powered pump and panels to the well, and with twelve hours of sunlight every day, we had clean water!

Like the Swahili proverb tells us, *"Maji ni uhai."* Our community understands well that "water is life." It is impossible to describe just how much importance clean water holds in places like our village, as well as the gift this well became to the community as it gave access to clean drinking water.

For the last fourteen years, the well has served our patients and staff and enabled us to place a tap outside of our gate to offer clean water to our neighbors. We love our neighbors, and we knew it mattered that we shared.

Every day, hundreds of women walk to Living Room's gate to fill their yellow jerry cans before placing them on their heads to return home. As a result, we have witnessed waterborne sicknesses in our community reduce significantly.

The gift of water has also strengthened our relationship with our neighbors. I recently heard one neighbor say, "There were so many diseases that people were suffering from, but right now we no longer have them because of clean water. We are seeing the community benefit from this as well as the hospice services."

* * *

A small prayer chapel was built at both of our Living Room campuses. We constructed our first chapel in Eldoret while the larger hospital was being built, and we felt it so represented who we are as a community that we made plans to build one at Kimbilio Hospice, too.

The buildings are hexagon in shape, with wooden beams for a ceiling. Exquisite Kenyan stained-glass windows wrap around the chapel. Shades of red, blue, green, yellow, and white reflect on those inside, offering the words in both English and Swahili that we so often need to be reminded of: faith, hope, love, and peace.

Another stained-glass window with a red cross in the center adorns the front of the chapel, and clear glass windows run along its walls above the stained glass, offering views into the garden.

The first time I entered the chapel in Eldoret, two days after arriving back in Kenya in 2019, I was overcome by its message, by the light shining through the colored glass. I sat down to see what the view would be like for a child or someone seated in a wheelchair.

It felt important that the chapel, a place of prayer, would be inclusive in this way. That everyone would understand it was a safe and sacred place for them to come. I had an overwhelming hope and desire as I lingered there: *May all feel welcome here.*

Two years later, on the day the second chapel was dedicated, Kimbilio choir's beautiful singing could be heard far and wide as the words declared, *"Ametukumbuka."* He has remembered us.

The choir wore matching t-shirts with the words, "Honouring lives, offering hope," plastered across their backs. It is the vision of Living Room that we can live in the most practical and sacred of ways, each and every day.

The singing continued in multiple languages, refrains repeatedly telling of the goodness of God. As I listened, I could almost hear the singing of all the patients we had cared for over the years joining in with the choir.

Sitting beside a five-year-old boy in his wheelchair, I was moved by the suffering held within his body, but even more so by the light that still filled his eyes. He sat, taking it all in, as if he knew the place was made for him.

The same was true for the former college student, now a patient, who sat next to the little boy. Cancer had already taken his left leg and threatened much, much more, but he stood to say, "God is good; this should be our daily word."

Patients and staff, sitting alongside one another, gave thanks for the gift of this space with enough room for everyone to come and belong, welcomed as they are. The brokenness was untellable, but so was the abundance of love.

* * *

One of the most beautiful things I've witnessed in Living Room's work is when a guest of Kimbilio shifts from being a patient to a host. It is something I didn't anticipate, but it has occurred again and again. Patients are cared for by our team and loved in the mundane of each day. When some have recovered, they want to extend the same care that was extended to them.

Who better for us to listen and learn from than those who came through our doors with their own unique stories of suffering? Those who ate our food, lied in our beds, were bathed, and had their dressings changed? Those who don't know Living Room simply as a vision, but instead have had a front row seat to the care provided day and night?

Muthoni, a mother living with HIV, was referred to Kimbilio because of an extensive, excruciating leg wound that just wouldn't heal. Muthoni's wound was painful but also psychologically tormenting—so much so that she wanted to cut off the leg.

She needed rest, proper nutrition and medication, and frequent dressing changes. She needed time—lots of it—for her leg to slowly heal. Our team encouraged her emotionally as, day by day, they provided the physical care she needed.

Each morning, Muthoni positioned herself with her leg elevated to sit in the garden among the children who were guests, helping to hold them, play with, and feed them. It wasn't required of her, but she did it with love and kindness. By the time Muthoni was ready to go home, we offered her a job to officially become a part of our caregiving team.

Becoming a host to other guests at Kimbilio meant reminding them of their value and worth, warmly welcoming them and tenderly caring for them. It meant, at times, to be the powerful voice that says, "I was once a patient, too. I was sicker than you are, but I got better. It took a long time, but I got better. Take your medicine. God loves you. Don't give up."

* * *

That same shift happened to me in 2017 when I went from being the host, the welcomer and helper, to a guest in a home when my family moved to Los Angeles for our boys' transplant season.

Much like Living Room's vision, hospitality was offered to us, not just in having a place to stay, but through the people who walked alongside us. In our darkest, most vulnerable times, we had hosts who kept offering us a safe place to rest, kept reminding us we were loved, welcome, and not alone.

We stayed together for much longer than any of us anticipated, as there were so many bumps along the way. Setbacks on some days felt disappointing, and other moments felt like the last straw.

We were messy and needy, and we came to the end of ourselves more than once. We didn't have a timeline to know how many days we'd stay or when we might go home.

It's a humbling journey to need. To receive. To feel depleted, dependent, uncertain, and exposed. Yet, at the same time, to experience such kindness and love. It wasn't owed to us in any way, and yet I will always be grateful it was extended.

When we returned home to Kenya in January of 2019, I understood so much better, from experience, from trial by fire, what it means to be a guest. What it feels like to be a mother advocating on behalf of my children, the vulnerability and strength in receiving the generosity of others.

As much as anything, I now know what it is to be *that* mama.

Who gets to determine
the limits of what is possible?
And, more importantly, for who?
Or what if? And what should be?
If rockets can land on Mars,
couldn't clean water be available to all?
If a disease is treatable somewhere,
then why not here too?
Maybe it's comparing apples to oranges—
or perhaps just a failure to see
that audacious things are
only absurd, impractical
until they come to be.

Chapter Seven

Impossible Things, Together

Some nine months after our family returned from California, surrounded by family and friends, I witnessed and cheered as our friend and fellow Kenyan, Eliud Kipchoge, became the first man to run a marathon in under two hours—a feat that many experts said could never be done. It was World Hospice Day, October 12, 2019.

The race was run along a tree-lined avenue on a brisk Saturday morning in Vienna, Austria. Everything about the event was calculated down to the second, and it had to be executed with perfection for Eliud to succeed at his dream of breaking two hours.

He would need to run for 26.2 miles at a pace of just under 4:35 minutes per mile. Thousands of spectators lined the route to cheer for Eliud and the team of forty-one pacemakers, while millions more watched from around the world.

A key factor in Eliud's success was a team of pacers who ran in a V-formation with him in the middle—five teams of seven pacers that alternately kept Eliud out of the wind. They followed a car that projected laser lines on the road to aid them in maintaining a precise pace.

As the final team of pacers neared the finish line, they slowed as the crowd's cheering swelled. Eliud completed his race in 1:59:40:2.

In the final seconds, we all knew he had succeeded and achieved the impossible. But it was the other runners' enthusiasm and unbridled joy, arms lifted to the sky, celebrating Eliud, that felt equally moving to me. They were all giving their very best for him to achieve the goal of the day.

So often, for someone to be a winner, everyone else has to lose. But on this special day, there was no ranking or order of first to last. No one had to compare themselves, or feel shame or regret for their position in the race. Everyone who participated worked, in sync, all together, toward a single goal.

It's hard to articulate all the implications we spectators felt in this moment. It wasn't just about watching superhuman-fast runners or breaking records. Yes, we gathered to witness and cheer for that, but there was more to it.

Eliud didn't give up when he was tired.

He didn't quit when it was hard.

He didn't stop trying after failed attempts.

His success required years of discipline and training, of imagining and reimagining what could be possible, and then with laser focus—literally—fighting for it.

Perhaps most moving was the fact that Eliud needed others to accompany him, and they did so in the most remarkable and inspiring of ways.

I stood with my family in a room full of people in David and Allison's home, in a country, on a continent, where the voices all around so often seem to shout, "You are poor. There will never be enough. Death always wins. You aren't good enough."

Much like Eliud's pacers, we were screaming in celebration, marked by joy in a way I hope to never forget. It was a moment of resistance, recognizing those limiting voices, which we too often listen to, were speaking lies.

Eliud's success, as well as the pacers who supported, protected, encouraged, and led him while they ran alongside him, felt prophetic, like the words my friend Susan wrote in response to the joy of the day:

"There is something about human achievement of this kind that sends electric hope through me. That we are designed for greatness. That we are powerful. That we are determined. That we can not only shatter records, but maybe we can also end world hunger, and ameliorate climate change, and find homes for foster youth and bring healing and compassion and hope and faith to a world that needs it. I am praying today for this kind of determination and perseverance to grow larger in my soul. That I can be a blessing to this world in more notable ways today than I was yesterday. That I can run the race before me with more confidence in the God I trust."

* * *

There's an African proverb that says, "If you want to go fast, go alone. If you want to go far, go together."

It's likely that Eliud would propose, especially in his situation, that you can go fast *and* far together. But there are many instances, especially living and working in community, where difficult things require both partnership and unhurriedness.

Patience doesn't always come easy to me, as I value efficiency and like to get from here to there without delay. But I also understand, from years of working in global health, that doing hard things together is a better way.

My pace isn't always the best or right speed, just as my ways aren't always the best approach, and I value the Kenyan leaders I work alongside who have helped guide me, time and again.

Similarly, when our children grew sick, friends and family graciously slowed down, interrupting their plans, taking their time and resources, to journey with us, even when no end was in sight.

Somewhere in the middle of transplant season, Mama Micah and I picked up a laminated sign from the teacher's supply store that read, "Difficult things take a long time. Impossible things take a little longer." We taped it onto the wall, and it became a slogan of sorts that we'd often refer to.

While Geoffrey was in the hospital, after he'd received his ten days of chemotherapy and the gift of his sister Sharon's bone marrow, there was a period of waiting, of watching for his white blood cell count to slowly rise from zero a little each day. The graft of Sharon's cells was in its infancy, fragile, but it was taking.

As I texted the daily lab reports to Baba and Mama Micah, she placed another sign on their refrigerator door, written in black and red marker: ANC 350, and then crossed off to read 480, followed by 740, and then 910. At the bottom of the sign, it read: "Go Geoffrey! Go Sharon!"

A community walked alongside Geoffrey, a little boy who had traveled the world, who we had grown to love in immeasurable ways.

When I think back on the chances of Geoffrey and Ryan ever receiving this treatment, it's mind boggling. And yet, somehow, it happened.

It wasn't accidental or haphazard. It required great intention and planning, navigating barriers of all kinds. But it happened.

* * *

Before we moved to Los Angeles, Dr. Jodi, a friend and pediatric transplant doctor, advised us, "You will need community to survive this."

While I couldn't yet understand the magnitude of her words, the intensity of what was before us, I knew the value of community. It's the vision Living Room was built upon—to be a community of compassion, understanding certain things cannot and should not be done or attempted alone. Difficult things, and even more so, impossible things, need to be done in community.

I trusted Dr. Jodi's words and leaned into them. I didn't know the details of *who* the community would be or what it might look like, but we chose to go to Los Angeles, to a place where I had lived before moving to Kenya.

In the most unexpected and beautiful of ways, we had our own team of pacers that surrounded us, hemming us in and encouraging each and every step along the way.

New friends and old friends alike linked arms with our family and didn't let go. They helped to hold us up. They cried with us and celebrated on so many days.

For all my life, I will cherish the ways they affirmed my little boys' lives. They told them, and us, again and again, with their words and actions: "Keep going— you're going to make it! Keep going—don't give up! Keep going—it won't stay dark forever!"

* * *

For eighteen years, I have had the immense privilege of journeying alongside Kibet and Karimi, a husband and wife who were among my first patients when I moved to Kenya. It's hard to fathom just how far we three have come, how much we have learned and created together, along the way.

Karimi can be found, on any given day, faithfully working at Living Room. She wears a uniform of scrubs and stands all of five feet tall, always with a bright smile on her face. Karimi folds mounds of hospital linens at Kimbilio Hospice, and she'll greet whoever comes into the room with great warmth as she continues in her work.

Her husband proudly stands at the gate of the hospice and salutes you as you enter and leave. The sash draped across his chest reads, "Here to serve."

Kibet knows well that by the time a guest arrives at the gate, they have walked a long and arduous road, often literally. Each guest comes with a unique story, with hopes and fears, with a failing body, and with the pain and suffering that goes along with advanced disease.

Our job, once they reach us, is to make sure they understand they are not alone, that we will walk with them. And Kibet understands it is his job to warmly welcome and direct each family bringing their loved one into our care.

His familiarity with being incurably sick, with feeling overlooked and undervalued, guides him in his work. He knows it is for such people that this little refuge known as Kimbilio was created.

On a warm afternoon in late December 2004, I couldn't have imagined any of this, for Kibet and Karimi or for me. Kibet was asleep under the shade of a banana tree, covered by a heavy, woolen blanket, his body ravaged by untreated disease. Little more than a skeletal frame remained.

A neighbor had requested for me to check on Kibet, and so I came. There was still much stigma and fear attached to AIDS at the time, and while everyone assumed Kibet had it, no one would say the word.

I had been living in Kenya only three months on the day we met, and I thought I knew how the story would go. I would make routine home visits to care for Kibet and Karimi. Within weeks, Kibet would die without a proper diagnosis, without an option of treatment.

The community would gather for Kibet's burial, and the problem of AIDS would continue its destructive and unchallenged pattern.

But a few days later, Kibet and I happened upon an HIV testing and treatment center in Turbo, a town only ten miles away. It had recently opened, and when I drove Kibet there, I thought it was a normal clinic.

That was the day I met Dr. Joe Mamlin. As we stepped into a room filled with HIV test kits, nutritional support, and antiretrovirals, all I saw was hope. Tears filled my eyes as I realized the dreams that I had been dreaming were smaller than God's plans for Kibet, for Karimi, and for thousands of others in our community.

After a few months of taking his daily cocktail of *dawa*—his anti-HIV medications—Kibet, along with many others from our community, experienced the Lazarus effect. People who had appeared to be dead were coming back to life.

It was not only the medicine that changed their lives. Working alongside a small but committed team of Kenyans who were passionate about the holistic care we provided our patients and their families, we witnessed the power of love tearing down the walls of fear and shame.

Five years later, in 2010, Living Room was just beginning, and Kimbilio Hospice was remarkably, although unintentionally, being built on land directly across from Kibet and Karimi's home. Kibet was a part of the construction team, pushing wheelbarrows filled with sand or cement back and forth.

Karimi would tell you she believes the vision of Living Room began when we met her husband under the shade of their tree. It all started with simple acts of mercy—one life at a time.

In 2019, on the evening our family arrived back to Kenya from LA, Kibet walked from his home to ours, part of the parade to receive us, now celebrating victory and life with us.

* * *

The Living Room story is one of years spent walking alongside our patients in the community we serve, believing hard things can be done together. This journey requires great humility, not assuming we know what is needed before we listen, before we sit in homes and understand, in part, the complexity of the unique lived experience.

We ask questions about the barriers people face that prevent them from accessing and affording treatment, or following through on taking their medicines, or going to the clinic. We listen to the impossible choices required of so many people each day in our community.

As with every guest who turns to us for hope, a twelve-year-old boy named Shadrack found his way to Kimbilio in late 2021, months after a tree climbing accident that left him paralyzed from the waist down. Shadrack arrived just as COVID-19 began to slow down.

He had extensive pressure ulcers and desperately needed nursing services and physical therapy.

In addition to the physical and emotional care we provided, Shadrack received tutoring from our teacher, Jacob. Once a guest of Kimbilio himself, Jacob sat beside Shadrack three mornings a week, each in their wheelchairs. Jacob taught reading, writing, and mathematics, but he also reminded Shadrack, again and again, of his value and worth. He reminded Shadrack there was still hope.

In Kenya, very few schools are wheelchair accessible, which meant when Shadrack was ready to leave Kimbilio, he wouldn't be able to continue with his education. This felt unacceptable to our team, so we dreamt of a way to break down the barriers for Shadrack and others who might follow. Living Room partnered with the leaders at a school within our community to make a path, both literally and logistically. They constructed ramps and walkways, as well as wheelchair accessible toilets and showers.

By the time Shadrack arrived at his new school with bright eyes and the widest grin imaginable, he drove himself around campus.

With wonder and tear-filled eyes, I followed behind Shadrack and the group of classmates welcoming him.

All I could think was, *This must be what Jesus meant when he said, "Let the children come to me."*

Through a caring community working together to include and ease the burden of one—much like pacers in formation taking on the full force of the wind so Eliud Kipchoge could cross the finish line—what had felt impossible was done.

Do we have room to love,
knowing the outcomes are uncertain?
Will we choose to try, to give our best,
even when it feels like it isn't enough?
Are we willing to care,
knowing love is
the cost and the reward?

Chapter Eight

Brave Love

When my babies were small, I spent countless hours carrying them nestled against my chest in a purple Ergo baby carrier. I'd sway side to side, shifting the weight from one foot to the other. Back and forth, like a grandfather clock's pendulum swinging in time. Tick-tock, tick-tock, tick-tock.

The swaying, like so much of motherhood, involved being present. Day by day, night after night. When no one was watching. When the baby was tired, and I was tired. When the baby was quiet, and all felt right in the world. In our home. In hospital rooms. As we walked through the neighborhood. Always, a gentle, quiet swaying.

This instinct to rock and soothe my baby also worked to calm my mind and body. I did it often, for so long, that even after I'd put my baby down, I'd still find myself swaying back and forth.

Long since my children have outgrown their carrier, I sometimes still gently rock from side to side, in the same familiar motion, as though my body, from countless hours of repetition, decides to do it for me. It quiets itself through the movement, regulating my nervous system.

Other times, I'll notice myself moving in this way to try and quiet the crying baby in the hospital's pediatric ward or as a response to the pain of someone nearby.

Love is a willingness to be present when it is uncomfortable, and a mother's love involves showing up with vulnerability for our children in whatever ways might be required of us. Like Brené Brown says, "The thing about vulnerability is when you feel uncertainty, when you feel risk, when you feel exposed, don't tap out. Stay brave."[13]

I used to think being brave meant being unafraid rather than what it actually is—showing up to face the fear and pain.

But somewhere in the middle of our transplant journey, knowing both the cost and the reward of love, I began saying, "Love makes us brave."

Through the lens of motherhood, I have come to see the world. It's both a hard-earned gift for the benefit of

---

13 *60 Minutes*, season 52, episode 27, Brene Brown, aired March 29, 2020, on CBS News, https://cbsn.ws/46teqzf.

my children and a growing compassion for other mamas and theirs.

* * *

In 2019, when the buildings were completed, and the staff of Living Room's hospital in Eldoret were hired and ready to provide patient care, very few patients came to the hospital for treatment. The vision was in place, and we had no doubt that the sick in our area desperately needed the services.

Like the line from a classic movie of my childhood, *Field of Dreams*, I had thought, "If you build it, they will come."[14] But they didn't come, at least not with the immediacy I imagined.

Weeks led to months, and the hospital had maybe five to ten of its forty-nine hospital beds filled. There were reasons for it—bureaucratic delays with the registration of the hospital and an accreditation process for the national health insurance fund that took a whopping two years instead of the two weeks we were initially promised.

In my heart, I believed the gap between where we were and where we hoped to go was small, but on numerous days, it felt impossible to bridge, no matter how hard

14 Robinson, Phil Alden. 1989. Field of Dreams. United States: Universal Pictures.

we tried. It was disheartening on so many levels to have such a beautiful space and team ready and to not fulfill its purpose to care for those suffering in sickness.

A few months into the waiting, I received a call from a doctor working at the government hospital in oncology. I had long worked with him in facilitating patient referrals to Kimbilio for hospice care. This colleague told me that their hospital had created a strategy to partner with private hospitals to help decongest the overcrowded hospital wards.

"As you know, we often have two or three patients share a bed on any given day. Living Room's name came up in a meeting as a potential partner to work with. I wanted to see if you would be interested in getting together to discuss further."

I was interested, indeed. We agreed to meet that week.

I was well acquainted with the overcrowding at the government hospital, as I did rounds with the palliative care team every Tuesday morning. Each week, some of the patients would be referred to Kimbilio for hospice care because of their advanced disease. I knew the names, faces, and the stories of many adults and children who had traveled far distances to receive cancer treatment.

One Tuesday morning during rounds, shortly after I returned to Kenya from our boys' treatment, I met a sixteen-year-old girl who had her heart set on finishing high school. Her favorite subjects were biology and chemistry. But as I stood beside her bed in the center of a busy hospital ward, quiet tears flooded her face.

She was being transferred to Kimbilio for hospice care.

The place felt congested with so many in need of help, the sounds of suffering all around. In the middle of the chaos, this young girl with a name and a story did not want to go with us. I didn't want her to need hospice care, either, but cancer had ravaged her body in such a cruel way that everything was shutting down.

She told us she wasn't afraid, just sad and disappointed. There weren't words to make any of it OK—so I didn't try.

I believe in hope and healing, in the mercy of a loving God. With the space between us, the only way I knew to extend this love was to be quiet and sit in the sadness, staying there, even if for a moment.

Was it possible, amid all the suffering, to offer a blessing? Not in a magical, weird sort of way, but as John O'Donohue writes, "the word blessing evokes a sense of warmth and protection; it suggests that no life is alone or unreachable."[15]

From within the silence of my heart, a mama's heart, I prayed: "May your going be sheltered and your welcome assured."[16]

* * *

After multiple meetings with doctors from the government hospital, we articulated a need together.

For Kenya's forty-five million people, cancer is the third leading cause of death, with an estimated 50,000 new cases of cancer and 33,000 deaths annually.[17] With few public cancer treatment centers in Kenya, patients must travel long distances to receive medical treatment and lack accommodation during treatment. At the second largest hospital in Kenya, Moi Teaching and Referral Hospital (MTRH), seventy percent of cancer patients travel more than sixty miles to receive care.

Patients do not always require admission to the hospital for their treatment, but they often lack housing during that time. They either have to travel long distances while sick, or they have to struggle to pay to stay at a

---

15 John O'Donohue, *To Bless the Space Between Us: A Book of Blessings* (New York: Doubleday, 2008), *xiii.*
16 Traditional Irish blessing.
17 Technical Team, "Cancer Kenya 2020 Country Profile," *World Health Organization,* January 1, 2020, https://bit.ly/44wROfw.

hotel. Instead, many patients and family members sleep in hospital corridors, in cars, or on the street.

If Living Room were to assist with lessening the load at MTRH, we would want to build a guesthouse. We talked of constructing a family care center in order to welcome children and their families going through cancer treatment. This had been a dream I had for Living Room before I knew firsthand how overwhelmingly scary and hard cancer treatment is, even in a best-case scenario.

As a mom, I can't begin to imagine sleeping on the floor of a crowded hospital corridor with my sick baby, waiting for another round of chemo.

I also still had the fresh muscle memory of what it is like to be far from home, longing and aching, desperate for my children to access the treatment they required, hoping that they would survive. I remembered the debilitating treatment that felt like another form of death, the side effects and pain, the exhaustion that never really went away.

And when reprieve was close, I recall how exhausting and impossible it felt to start again. To be lovingly welcomed into a home, so far away from ours, by a family that made room for us to come and stay—I wanted that for every mama going through similar crises.

So, I told the hospital team, "Someday, I believe we'll build this guesthouse, but even now, we have space for the children and their guardians to come. We have beds today and a loving team who is ready to welcome them! While we continue to develop the hospital and dream of constructing this guesthouse, we'd be honored to welcome these families. Let them come and stay. We'll take care of them."

* * *

While these discussions were still under way, we invited the Vice President of Kenya, along with a thousand of our neighbors, to celebrate the official opening of Living Room's hospital in Eldoret. The national media accompanied the dignitaries to broadcast the events of the day.

Our staff gave a quick tour to the Vice President, Ministry of Health Officials, Governor, and other leaders, and we proceeded to the tents, where we cut a cake decorated with green mint icing to celebrate ten years of Living Room.

I ate my slice of cake just prior to giving a speech. I tried my best to abide by the protocols required but mostly spoke with conviction about the vision God had given us to do Living Room's work with compassion and excellence. After the speech, the Vice President shook my hand, and I sat down. Ella promptly climbed onto my lap.

"Mom," she said, with a look of confusion in her eyes, "What is wrong with your mouth?"

Looking at Allison, I whispered, "Is there something on my face?"

She slowly nodded. "It looks like you're wearing green lipstick."

I had the honor of addressing the country, its leaders, and our neighbors with green-stained lips and teeth, thanks to the frosting on the cake.

* * *

Days before my addressing the nation with green teeth, our sweet Alice had a sickle cell crisis. Complications led to her being admitted to the ICU that Sunday night. Her decline was fast and scary, and as I spoke that Tuesday about Living Room's vision of providing access to affordable healthcare to the most vulnerable, the ache of her suffering was in my gut.

Thankfully, the hospital called Titus during the ceremony to let us know Alice was being discharged from the ICU to a normal hospital bed. He missed most of the celebration to be with her.

During my speech, I shared how we were celebrating many dreams coming true in the official opening of this facility. "I am grateful for the beautiful hospital that has been created, for the serene gardens and the sacred chapel that fill this space. But the real measure of our success will be in the patient care we provide," I told the crowd.

That afternoon, Alice was transferred to Living Room to recover under the care of our team until she was well enough to come home.

* * *

Among the many books I love reading to my children, one stands out. It's called *I'll Take Care of You.*[18] Its colorful illustrations and beautiful themes of care and community are tender and filled with hope.

The first page has one lonely sentence: "Once there was a tiny seed. So small in the great big world, it felt lost and lonely."

The sky, water, and earth show up to welcome the seed and say, "Don't be afraid. I'll take care of you." With enough time, the seed grows into a magnificent apple tree.

---

18 Maria Giraldo and Nicoletta Bertelle, *I'll Take Care of You* (San Francisco: Blue Dot Press, 2022).

One night, when the tree meets a bird in need of help, it offers its branches as a shelter and says, "Stay here and build your nest in my branches. I'll take care of you."

Within the safety of the tree, the little bird builds her nest and lays her egg. When the chick hatches, the mother says, "I'll take care of you."

A time comes when all the apples are gone from the tree, all but one. A tiny seed remains, and the mama bird, full circle, returns to say to the weeping tree. "Don't worry," she says. "I'll take care of our tiny one."

The book ends as the bird waits with hope, singing with all her heart until a tiny shoot of new life appears.

Whenever I read this story, I'm reminded of our family's parallel journey. One that goes something like this: Once there was a tiny baby boy wrapped tightly in a pink blanket. So small without his mother in the great big world, he felt lost and lonely.

A mama and daddy looked upon the baby boy, and their hearts swelled with love. The mama said to the baby, "Don't be afraid. I'll take care of you." And she welcomed him into their home.

The baby was adored and safe to grow, until, one day, the pain from a terrible sickness became too much for him. A big sister saw how sick her baby brother and bigger brother were. She said, "Don't be afraid. I'll take care of you. As far as we need to go, we will fly."

And so, the sister and brothers and their family flew across the entire world, until they arrived at a house the same color as sunshine. The owners saw that the family needed a safe place to rest and said, "Stay here as long as you need. We'll take care of you."

The sister and brothers' family lived in the warmth and kindness of the openhearted home for 477 days, patiently aching and waiting together for new life to come. All along the way, they said to one another, "Don't be afraid. Difficult things take a long time. Impossible things, just a little longer."

When the healing found its way, they all took heart, knowing it was time to fly across the world again. Love would lead them back home, and it did. There were still impossible things that needed doing, but brave love, the family had learned, would guide their way.

Sometimes love, at any moment, on any given day,
invites us to inconveniently go another way.
To turn left instead of right.
To cross the road, to sit tight.
To notice what has always been right there.
Choosing to look, listen, and care.

Chapter Nine

Interruption

I received a pair of cozy slippers from my sister for Christmas in 2019. Neither she nor I had any way of knowing just how much I'd end up wearing them in the year to come. I went into 2020, like so many other people, feeling like it was a season of vision, but not in the ways the year would bring its own sense of clarity, chaos, and uncertainty.

At the start of 2020, I was hopeful that we'd overcome the delays and setbacks we had experienced in opening Living Room's new hospital. There were so many goals to achieve and plans in place. My floral printed "12-Month Productivity Organizer" for that year had so many things scheduled in blue ink, and like everyone, everywhere, my plans were pretty on paper but not to be lived out.

Titus, the kids, and I were finally finding our way back to some sense of normalcy after the trauma of treatment and the readjusting to life and culture in Kenya. For the first time in my fifteen years of living in Kenya, my entire family—my mom and dad, my siblings and nephew—was coming in June to visit our home and Living Room, then going on safari together to the Maasai Mara.

Mama and Baba Micah, Micah, and several other dear friends from our time in LA were planning a month-long trip to participate in a camp with some of our Kenyan runners.

Early in February, Titus and I traveled for a weekend getaway with Dr. Joe and his wife, Sarah Ellen, as well as a team of other doctors. We visited a research center where elephants, cheetahs, and all sorts of magical wildlife roam. I was excited to see Joe and Sarah Ellen, now in their mid-80s. They were just visiting, as they had returned to the States in 2019. We had a wonderful time together, exploring the beauty of the land with these dear friends.

Sitting by a campfire on the final night of the weekend getaway, watching as the sun set, I vividly remember one of the senior doctors saying, "I've been following this virus in China and am feeling concerned about it. I have

N-95 masks, in case they are needed—it's making me nervous."

Around the same time, the news from Italy started to paint a picture of something much grimmer than just the flu. A doctor friend wrote that she had been watching what was happening there and was very concerned about what was coming to the States and the entire world. "I don't think the healthcare system is going to be able to handle this," she shared. "We must figure out how to slow the spread down."

Living Room had started major renovations on Kimbilio Hospice. This significantly reduced the number of patients we had in our care. At Living Room's hospital in Eldoret, we still only had a handful of patients.

In February, our leadership team began to have meetings, trying to prepare our response to this unfamiliar virus. What resources could we put in place? PPE? How could we protect and support our staff? Our patients? Our families? Our neighbors?

By early March, we got wind of the hype about the toilet paper shortage in the US. Ella, six at the time, responded by making a video for friends and family in which she explained, "People are buying so much toilet paper. You can't use too much toilet paper, or there won't be enough for everyone to have some."

True. What was also true were her insights most kids in the US wouldn't think of. Ella continued, "If you run out, people will need to use leaves instead. Just be careful in choosing leaves, not to use the poison ivy ones."

I watched events unfolding Stateside, paying attention as orders to shelter in place and practice social distancing were being implemented. I knew COVID-19 was on its way, if it wasn't already in Kenya.

Kenya's first case of COVID was confirmed on March 13, kicking off daily reports from Kenya's Ministry of Health. With limited access to testing, they'd report the number of new cases each day based on location, hospitalizations, deaths, and recoveries. Schools were closed, and students were sent home indefinitely, with no online schooling options for most.

Our own version of "stay at home" orders were implemented, and anyone who tested positive for COVID was required to stay at designated isolation locations. It didn't take long before Kenya's airspace was closed for all commercial flights, and no road travel was permitted between counties. Churches weren't allowed to gather in person, and weddings were banned.

On March 24, we received orders to suspend Living Room's mortuary services. Of all the things COVID would shut down, I didn't imagine our funeral home would be one of them, but the government didn't want large groups of people gathering around the death and burial of their loved ones. If someone died, they were to be buried immediately.

Like so many places in the world, when people in Kenya were ill with other sicknesses or needed follow-up medical care for already existing conditions, they were afraid to go to the hospital or to their clinics. Many people defaulted in taking the medications they needed for their other diseases.

In addition to all the complexities of COVID-19, we had heavy rains across Kenya, causing displacement, flooding, landslides, and death. We were even told to be on watch for hippos in the Kipkaren River.

And if things weren't already bizarre enough, Kenya was also experiencing its worst locust invasion in seventy years. I cringed when a BBC article entitled, "The Biblical Locust Plagues of 2020," popped up in my news feed. The article detailed the ability of a swarm of eighty million locusts to consume the food of 35,000 people a day.[19] This was also coming our way? Seriously, you couldn't make this stuff up.

---

19 David Njagi, "The Biblical Locust Plagues of 2020," *BBC*, August 6, 2020, https://bbc.in/3O9zbJf.

This new season was scary and shocking to experience. So many unknowns made the desire to protect one another feel urgent.

There was also the element of a world interrupted: the inability to make reliable plans or have a sense of control over our day-to-day choices posed another level of discomfort.

Sure, there were the early days of baking bread, playing board games, and building puzzles, but the adjustments to nearly all things in person being cancelled—thought to be temporary at first—lasted longer than anyone predicted or imagined.

At the beginning of the pandemic, there was some sense of unity, that we'd all work to protect one another, trying to get through it together. It helped me to watch "Some Good News" with John Krasinski, and laugh, cry and be inspired.

For many, the adjustments weren't just inconvenience—they were trying to survive COVID on top of the already daily struggle to survive. I was captivated by the words of a young man from Nairobi talking about COVID-19 and all the changes required by the government to try and curb the spread. "Please stop talking about a new normal," he said. "For those of us who wake up every day in the slums to look for food, all we are trying to do is survive. This has always been our normal."

* * *

For Living Room, difficult decisions needed to be made, but there wasn't enough information to make them amid the confusing trends and scary statistics.

I felt an invitation from God to be faithful to what was in front of us.

I returned to one of the mantras that had carried me during some of our darkest days of Ryan's transplant. At a time when complications had arisen and my mind spun with what might come next, my dear friend Sarah sent a message that my soul needed to receive: "*Don't get ahead of God.*"

In 2020, with troubles all around, I leaned again into it. *Don't get ahead of God.* I set aside my lofty goals and calendared events to focus on what was right in front of me.

Not looking too far ahead, I once again felt nudged to ask the guiding questions: What might it look like to love today? And then, to ask again tomorrow and the following day. What might hope look like in the middle of the story, when we're not guaranteed a specific outcome?

What does it look like to do justly now? To love mercy today? To accompany the poor in this season, fighting for health and wholeness? To not look away from those who are hurting, but to enter in, even if from six feet away, believing that God will be nearby?

I asked myself derivatives of those questions many times throughout the year.

What does it look like to love when schools are closed and I'm quarantined with five children in my house, when I'm tired and afraid, when the hospitals need new things or different things than we expected for this year, and the hospice is running differently?

What does it look like to love when resources feel limited, and needs are so many? With widespread flooding and over eight hundred thousand people displaced? What could social distancing look like for them, when so many in poverty live in overcrowded spaces and neighborhoods where space is a luxury? How do you tell the poor to stay at home when they are already trying to survive on less than a dollar a day?

These words began ringing through my head: "Do not love with words alone, but with actions and in truth" (see 1 John 3:18).

In that season, there were days when love looked like identifying neighbors who had food insecurity and providing maize and beans for five hundred families in our community. David Tarus worked with the local chief to determine five hundred families with the greatest needs. He blessed those who walked to pick up their bag of food with, "*Lisha watoto,*" feed your children, and, "*Amani ya Yesu,*" the Peace of Jesus.

On one of the days we distributed the food, I stood to the side and looked on for a moment, overwhelmed by the condition of the world, by the hunger in our neighborhood. I began to cry, and then an old song I often sing to my children began to rise within me.

I hummed until I quietly sang the words, "He's got the whole world in his hands, the whole world in his hands. He's got the whole world in his hands, the whole world in his hands." I believed this to be true—that God has me and all that I love within his hands.

In the midst of the hard and uncertainty, we can choose to find ways to love. We can experience God's nearness in suffering. In our exhaustion and disconnection, we can be gracious and kind to ourselves as we find creative ways to extend the same kindness and generosity to our neighbors.

* * *

In May 2020, we received a report that my dad was very sick with advanced heart failure. Kenya's airspace was still closed, so all I could do to be with my family was to Zoom in to the ache of my family's crisis. From the other side of the world, I tried to understand what was happening and read medical reports navigating getting my dad's care.

In November, after the airspace reopened, Titus and I traveled with the kids to California to spend time with my dad. Upon finishing our required two-week quarantine, Dad's symptoms were getting worse, and we had him admitted to the hospital. Because of COVID restrictions, though, we had to just drop him off outside a white tent. He was severely short of breath. We were heartbroken to just leave him.

The echocardiogram showed my dad's heart function had rapidly deteriorated and was severely impaired. The doctors released him the next day, basically saying there was nothing more they could do.

Dad asked us to put up the Christmas tree on November 15, that year. The weight in the room was heavy and sad. Jodi, Josh, and I had always been children in this home, but that week, we had to make grown-up decisions around my dad's care. This transition felt like too much, too soon.

We wanted more time with Dad, many more Christmases, and it didn't seem like we were going to get them.

We called Baba Micah, who happens to be a renowned emergency medicine physician, and he advised us to get a second opinion at UC Davis. Jodi and I drove Dad to Sacramento, two and a half hours away. To protect our dad, we wore masks while he sat in the passenger seat, unsuccessfully trying to catch his breath.

Despite the entire back seat being open, I sat in the middle, the place I feel most comfortable as the middle child. But I was no longer a child, and ready or not, I was stepping into the role of advocate and nurse on my dad's behalf.

At our appointment, a kind cardiologist admitted Dad to UC Davis Medical Center. There, the heart failure team worked to get additional testing, to pull excess fluid, and to adjust medications.

On the Tuesday of Thanksgiving week, Mom and I went back to Sacramento to pick him up. We celebrated Thanksgiving in my parents' garage with the door open, set on protecting one another with distance, while also not wanting to miss these moments.

Like everyone, everywhere, we were trying to navigate the complexities of life and family in the middle of a pandemic that was threatening and stealing so much life.

* * *

When Living Room first got its start, I asked my dad if he would help register the organization in the US. He did and would eventually become the Executive Director of the ministry. He led alongside me for a decade. Now, he was too sick to continue with this work. His retirement was a necessary transition but still another loss and change to navigate.

That year ended up not being Dad's last Christmas with us. Mom and Dad celebrated fifty years of marriage in May 2021. Dad was referred to Stanford for a potential heart transplant, but to the surprise of his doctors and all of us, his heart had markedly improved. The medications were working. It wasn't a complete healing that no longer required medical treatment, but it provided us with an unexpected gift of time. To us, that was a miracle.

June the next year, two years after my family had planned to visit us in Kenya, they finally came. It had long been my dad's dream for our whole family to be in Africa together, a dream that even a year earlier was impossible for many reasons.

Until my mom, dad, sister, brother-in-law, nephew, and brother were all on airplanes bound for Nairobi, I didn't allow myself to fully believe they were coming. My sister, Jodi, sent me a text message as they took off. It was the middle of the night in Kenya, but I didn't care. I woke Titus up with tears streaming down my face with excitement. "They're coming, Titus! They're actually coming."

We had two weeks of my family seeing our lives from the ground. Our home. The work we do. The people who fill our lives. The dirt paths which make up our roads—we walked them together.

They planted trees to the sound of our team singing to welcome them and received farewell gifts to another song when we said good-bye. We finished the trip with a few days together at the Maasai Mara, enchanted by the beauty and wonder of the place as well as the gift of experiencing it together.

That time was even more precious after Dad's health scare and the pandemic. The pandemic gave all of us a gift—a deeper appreciation for time with loved ones. We recognized that, for many, the pandemic involved someone they love dying without getting to be with them or say good-bye.

Estimates put the number of deaths related to COVID-19 well into the millions. When I think of the magnitude of that loss, I am not convinced we can grieve on that large a scale. To reconcile what was actually taken from us, we must break down the loss to the sum of its parts.

We can mourn the death of one forty-four-year-old single mother of three. Plus one seventy-two-year-old farmer in Kenya who still loved to hold his wife's hand after forty-four years of marriage. Plus, one thirty-five-year-old ER nurse in New York who loved her work but also vanilla ice cream and her golden retriever. Plus, one ninety-two-year-old dearly loved grandmother of six. Plus, one twenty-six-year-old man living on the streets of Los Angeles, his mother still praying he'd come back home. And the addition continues, one plus one, over and again until we reach millions loved, millions lost.

Only then, when the statistics of those who have suffered become less about numbers and more about the faces of friends and family and neighbors, can we begin to answer the question: What does love ask of me today? Now? Whether in the midst of a global pandemic or on the most ordinary of days.

What brave, simple thing can I do today to help ease someone's suffering?

"It's too dark," he shouts.
"Me needs light."
But no flickers can be found,
at least not tonight.

Terror is close by,
befriended by uncertainty.
Waiting for what, I cannot remember.
The cry of "How long?" resembles "Come quickly."

What if silence isn't the same as absence,
and You are closer than I feel?
Nothing, not even death and this darkness,
can separate or steal
me from your love.

Chapter Ten

Life Found in the Dark

A t Living Room, as in life, healing is often slow work. It involves caring not just for the parts of us that are acutely ill but allowing time to do its work in our whole being—physically, emotionally, and spiritually.

I've been learning this in my own healing process since returning from our transplant journey and also drawing encouragement from the stories of Living Room guests who illustrate this slow but miraculous work of healing.

"I used to be angry all the time, but I am no longer angry," Jacob shared from his wheelchair, his quiet confidence filling the room. He spoke to fifty-plus visitors who had come from near and far to celebrate the opening of the second Living Room site in early 2019. He narrated the long story of his journey with Living Room and how it transformed his life.

"I had already given up by the time I arrived at Kimbilio, but if you go out to the walkway, the words *Honouring Life* are inscribed at one end and *Offering Hope* are at the other. This is the care I received here."

I sat among the visitors listening to Jacob speak, remembering when he first arrived at Kimbilio in 2011. How sad and withdrawn and hopeless he was. I didn't know anything about him or his story when I saw him sitting on the veranda in his wheelchair. When I greeted him in Swahili, he replied in English, his affect flat, letting me know he wasn't interested in talking to me.

I'd come to learn that Jacob had been a teacher in Nairobi, a *kali* one, very strict, as he'd say. One night, thieves violently broke into his home, shot and killed his seventeen-year-old nephew, and then shot Jacob. A bullet lodged in his spinal column, leaving him paralyzed from the waist down. The thieves had wanted electronics, more than just his television, but Jacob didn't have more to give.

Jacob spent the next eight months in a public hospital in Nairobi. He developed extensive bedsores. The wounds became so large and infected, Jacob was certain he would die. He *wished* he would die.

Before coming to Kimbilio, his neighbors told him that the hospice was a place where people come when there's nothing left to do for them, and that they don't usually come back home. "I am dying anyway," he told them. "I think I can do it there."

In addition to the physical and psychological trauma that Jacob experienced, he also felt he had lost his purpose and identity. He had lost his ability to be a breadwinner for his family.

When Jacob arrived at Kimbilio, he wanted to hide, to disappear. He'd often cover his face with the blanket, refusing to speak with the caregivers and clinical team, refusing to leave his bed or to eat the food that was served.

He tells of one caregiver, Victoria, who just wouldn't give up on him. She'd come into the room and encourage him to eat, asking if he wanted any special foods that she could prepare for him. "God still loves you, Jacob," she'd say, "and we want you to live."

And then, she would give him a piece of chicken.

For months, day after day, the Living Room team provided holistic care. Nurses diligently cleaned his wounds, turning him every two hours in his bed. They brought him meals or a cup of chai, lifted him in and out of his wheelchair, provided physical therapy, and offered tips for increased mobility and strength.

Perhaps most significantly, we provided space for Jacob to grieve his losses, and we mourned with him, sitting with him and loving him.

Still, Jacob's wounds were too extensive to heal by themselves. They were clean and well cared for, but we needed additional help. The day I accompanied Jacob and his wife to a hospital in Eldoret to see if he could have surgery to close the wounds, a film team following Jacob's story interviewed us in the hospital driveway.

"We just came out from meeting with a couple of surgeons," I said to the cameras, "and they were able to look at Jacob's wounds and said that it's possible to do these flap repairs, which is so important. I don't know how Jacob's feeling, but I'm feeling hopeful."

Uncharacteristic of him at the time, Jacob interrupted me. "I think there's some hope, too. They're going to heal."

I looked at Jacob and paused, surprised. I felt this monumental shift toward hope happening in a single moment. In truth, the moment was built upon months of moment-by-moment choices to love and affirm Jacob's worth.

I continued, "We've seen this so many times before— the need to fight for justice, the need to fight for people like Jacob who have become a part of our Living Room family."

For months, our team had advocated and spoken up for Jacob, when his presence was unnoticed, his voice unheard. We needed to work on his behalf for justice and for his health and healing, for his wholeness. Living Room raised the funds required for Jacob to get the series of surgeries he needed for his wounds to heal.

Dramatic transformation occurred in Jacob's life. He didn't walk again, but the light that shines through his eyes, silent but undeniable, narrates a story of resilience and hope.

Here, in a room filled with visitors, Jacob now spoke for himself, articulating a renewed purpose—to advocate on behalf of those who are differently-abled. As Jacob shared his story with our visitors, his voice strong and his message resounding, he smiled and said, "If you want to see what Living Room is about, just look at me. I am Living Room's greatest champion."

Sitting beside Jacob, listening attentively, was eleven-year-old Chepkoech, a guest of Living Room since 2017. An accident with a kerosene lamp in early 2016 had severely burned her legs, after which the lack of access and affordability of treatment resulted in excruciating, insufferable pain. By the time Chepkoech arrived at

Kimbilio Hospice, her legs were contracted into her chest, her skirt stuck to her open wounds.

Chepkoech's spirit was equally broken. On her first day with us, Chepkoech shared with our clinical director, Rachel, "I am an orphan. Who is going to listen to me when I cry?"

Rachel lovingly replied, "Look at me, Chepkoech. I am your mother. The way I treat my child is how I will treat you. We love you and will be here for you."

Chepkoech explained how she felt like God was punishing her and it was her fault that she had been burned.

Again, with great compassion, Rachel looked her in the eyes and spoke these words of truth: "Chepkoech, it was an accident. You are a child of God, and he does not burn his kids. God loves you, and he is going to heal you."

On that first day, Chepkoech didn't believe that hope was possible. Much like Jacob, she didn't know that healing could come her way. The girl sitting in the front of this room, however, was nothing like the image of the sorrow-filled, broken-bodied patient who had arrived at Kimbilio Hospice nearly two years earlier.

Jacob's and Chepkoech's journeys contained many parallels. Both arrived at Kimbilio Hospice with extensive wounds that seemed as though they would never heal, their hopelessness so pronounced, it was palpable.

As a guest of the Living Room, Chepkoech received daily holistic care, just like Jacob. She also underwent several surgeries. Slowly, as her pain lessened and wounds healed, life and hope returned to her eyes.

Chepkoech eventually regained the ability to walk, jump, and play.

Months after arriving at Kimbilio Hospice, Chepkoech shared with one of our caregivers that she was afraid she was falling behind in school. Our team invited Jacob, who had returned home to his wife and sons, to join the Living Room staff as Chepkoech's private tutor.

"That was the best moment of my life," Jacob told the room full of visitors. "I got to teach again and give back because of the service that was given to me."

Jacob, the teacher who was forced into early retirement, and Chepkoech, the diligent student, formed a deep bond, created by similar hardships that led them into deepest despair before rediscovering hope and purpose.

Jacob concluded in front of the gathering, "I asked Chepkoech what she wants to be when she grows up. She told me, 'I want to be a surgeon.' She will be a surgeon," he declared. "I will see to it that she becomes a surgeon."

* * *

Someone once asked Ryan, if he could have any superpower, what he would choose. My mama's heart swelled at his answer: love. Love is an essential part of all that we do at Living Room, and without a doubt, it's the most mysterious and transformative tool we have.

We are far from perfect but always longing to grow in love.

While Jacob and Chepkoech's stories are filled with extreme hardship, and both have carried the weight of suffering and sadness a long way, I don't believe it is helpful to compare one person's suffering to another. To separate their vulnerabilities from ours. In this world, there are troubles of many kinds. There are hard and horrible things that will break our hearts.

None of us are immune to it.

There are seasons where everything feels dark, and there is no way to see the next step ahead. We sit and wait, aching and longing for a glimpse of light, for some sort of horizon to ground and guide us.

But there is no prescriptive timeline to loss and grief, to pain and disappointment.

* * *

On a Tuesday in late September 2021, my book, *From Beyond the Skies,* officially launched. Our staff and patients gathered to celebrate with my family and me. It was a remarkable day, filled with singing and dancing, planting of trees, sharing a meal, and remembering all the ways God had been with us on this incredible journey.

At the time, I started describing the book as my "long letter," written for my children and all who had walked alongside us.

Toward the end of the book launch celebration, Jacob wheeled himself to the front of the chapel and asked me a question, one to which he already knew the answer. "Juli, what does the cover of your book mean?"

The cover image shows a silhouette of two little boys holding hands and standing in the middle of a night sky filled with stars and a crescent moon. On the horizon, you can see the sun beginning to rise.

I explained that the cover was about our family's journey with the boys' treatment and being a world away from home as we searched for a cure for their sickle cell disease.

While talking, I sensed the distance between the me who wrote the book and the me getting to experience its release. A slow healing had been taking place in me, in my family—one that was impossible to see daily, but over time, incrementally, I trusted it was happening.

Jacob looked me in the eye with a depth of knowing, as if to welcome me to the hard-earned, you-get-it club no one ever wants to be a part of.

He shook his head as if to disagree. "Juli, the cover of your book represents that life can be found in the dark. I know because it is what happened to me, too."

The changed me couldn't agree more.

To all who are hurting, troubled, afraid,
it's hard to know what to do with spring.
Listen, notice, leave room for the loss.
As blooms burst, trees bud,
birds begin to sing,
The grimmest nights are fading away.
There's an ache the beauty is awakening.
The fragile new life beside still bare limbs—
untamed, unhurried,
hope is in the waiting.

Chapter Eleven

Stubborn Hope

"What is the word for *hope* in Kalenjin?" I ask David Tarus on an early Thursday morning as we drive to work at Living Room's hospital in Eldoret. It's an hour-long commute filled with rolling hills and exquisite, rural landscapes, and random cows, chickens, and pigs along the way.

The closer we get to Eldoret, the more people and cars there are. The fields of green are gradually replaced with roadside shops and *jua kali* markets—informal businesses, like small carpentry shops, metal works, car repairs, and cobblers. Closer still, the small shops are replaced by bigger, more developed concrete buildings.

"Kamang'unet," David says. He says it again slowly, pronouncing each syllable, "Ka-ma-ng'u-net," asking me to repeat after him.

I want to learn the word itself, but I also desire to understand what it means conceptually within the language, within the world.

I find that words translated and explained from another language can bring a fresh perspective. I am in a season where certain, familiar words like *hope* and *blessing* seem vague and cheapened by misuse, but they also feel important, warranting a renewed search for their meaning.

And so, I ask, "We use the word *hope* all of the time, but what is it? When we say we are offering hope at Living Room, what are we really offering?"

David entertains my unrelenting questions. "Hope is more than a wish," he tells me. "It's like, you don't know when help will come, but you keep holding on believing it will arrive."

I pause to process. "I've long thought of hope as an aching and waiting, an expectation that what is wrong— all that is wrong—will one day be made right," I suggest. "We don't control the when or the how. And there isn't certainty of a specific outcome."

* * *

The puzzle on the kitchen counter captured the end of 2021 quite well for my family. I didn't intend to ring in the new year in California, working on Geoffrey's 300-piece puzzle by myself. But at 12:01 a.m., as fireworks went off throughout the neighborhood, only 299 pieces were in place.

I searched for the last one, wanting the picture to be complete. Wanting something, anything, to be simple. Nice and neat. Predictable. Controlled.

The piece was missing. I went to bed knowing I needed to let it go.

Titus was ten thousand miles away in Kenya. A dear uncle of his had suddenly passed, so Titus went home ahead of the children and me to be with his family. We were supposed to follow this week, leaving one home in California to go to our other. Instead, all three little ones and I were in isolation, trying to recover from the nastiness of COVID-19.

The planner in me wanted to know when we could go, wanted to make sure all the logistics of getting from here to there were in place. But there was much more to it than that. I wanted to know that we'd be OK, that the New Year would be less chaotic and divisive and scary than the world we had known over the past several years.

Two weeks later, after a series of COVID tests that needed to be negative and timed just right to get results within the allotted period required by Kenya's Ministry of Health, I stood in a line at LAX with my three children and a trolley of luggage stacked high.

We were ready to be home with Titus.

On the way to the airport, Geoffrey had nonchalantly said, "I told my hand, 'Wake up hand.' It's so sleepy."

At the time, my eye caught Mama Micah's. "I don't like that," she said under her breath. We asked Geoffrey a few more questions and then tried to let it go. *Maybe it's a strange leftover symptom of COVID*, I thought.

But while waiting to check in, Geoffrey started to have stroke-like symptoms.

I immediately sent a text to the Herberts. As medical practitioners, Baba Micah (Mel) and Mama Micah (Mary) understood the gravity of my message.

Mary had dropped us off at the airport barely thirty minutes earlier and was probably somewhere on the 405, heading back to Woodland Hills.

Mel was the first to respond. "What are G's symptoms?"

"He's saying his left hand and foot are sleepy. Strength seems to be OK."

"Left or both sides?"

I pushed the trolley a few more feet forward. "Originally, he was saying left, but now he's saying both. I'm getting ready to check in. Should I wait?"

My mind flooded with thoughts. *I don't want to stay. I don't want him to have a stroke on an airplane. I don't want him to have a stroke at all. I don't want the possibility of disaster to be the script for the day. I need Geoffrey to be safe.*

We reached the check-in desk, and I handed our passports to the agent.

"How many bags?"

"Four."

The agent was busy on her screen when Mel texted again. "Obviously, he is still at risk for stroke due to abnormal vessels from sickle cell. This is so hard—if he has a stroke, you don't want to be on a plane!"

As the agent asked me to place our suitcases on the scale, Mel wrote again. "Talked with the docs on call. They say don't go. If it's upper and lower, he needs to be seen."

In my gut, I already knew these words to be true.

"I'm sorry," I told the agent. "I need to take an emergency phone call." I didn't have the clarity or bandwidth to explain anything further. She handed me our passports, and I told my little ones to step aside.

Mel texted again. "Mary is heading back to LAX. I can meet you at UCLA."

I tried to maneuver our luggage, guide the kids, and help Geoffrey walk to a spot away from the crowded check-in line.

Ella started to cry. She was angry and sad and already knew before I said a word. "We aren't going home, are we? Again! We're never going home. I want to see my daddy."

Ryan joined in. "Me wants my daddy. Me wants to go home. To Kenya."

"I know," I assured them, trying to stay as calm as possible. "I want to go, too, but Geoffrey's not feeling well, and we need to take him to see his doctors. He's more important than us traveling today."

I didn't have the right words or enough hands for what the moment required—to carry the children, to push our luggage through the airport, back to the curb. To pivot from traveling home to Kenya today and instead navigate whatever this might be.

I looked at Ella, tears streaming down her face. "It's OK to be upset, Ella, but I need you to help me. Please hold Ryan's hand and pull this bag." I placed Geoffrey on top of the suitcases on the trolley, and we made our way back outside.

All three children were crying now, and I wasn't far behind.

I had them sit down on the sidewalk and gave each a peanut butter sandwich Mary had packed for our trip. I called our travel agent requesting help to cancel the tickets. Again.

But since we were already checked in, she couldn't do it. She told me I had to go back inside to sort it out.

"I can't go back inside," I told her, fighting a lump in my throat. "I'm taking my son to the hospital. It's like he's having a stroke."

I hated saying those words in the present tense. She assured me she'd try to help, and we hung up the phone.

Mama Micah arrived moments later. Like watching a video in reverse order, we placed the suitcases, one by one, into the trunk, and the kids crawled back into their car seats. "The stroke team has been activated and are waiting for us," Mama Micah whispered to me.

We started the drive to UCLA Medical Center, a place we've been to hundreds of times before. I leaned my head against the headrest, my eyes wide open. On behalf of all of us, Ella started to cry again, and Ryan joined her. Everything within me wanted the hard and scary parts of our story to be only memories of the past.

Baba Micah met us at the UCLA emergency department. As he picked Geoffrey up out of his car seat, I turned to Ella and Ryan, saying something like, "I love you. We will come home as soon as we can."

"Thank you," I whispered to Mama Micah. Tears wanted to rise, but I couldn't let them overflow. Not now.

A team of doctors and nurses was waiting to assess Geoffrey. Within minutes, they drew labs, checked and measured his vital signs, and started an IV. It was all scary, both in present time and in the memory of this familiar place and people that both saved our boys and left us with many scars.

Geoffrey began to cry inconsolably. Before I had time to comfort him, he was whisked down a white hallway for an MRI scan. The team added meds to his IV to help him relax, and with that, they rolled Geoffrey into the room while Mel, Britt (another ER doc and friend of ours), and I waited in the hallway, leaning against a wall.

"Are you OK?" Mel asked, shaking his head in disbelief.

I just nodded.

Before Geoffrey's MRI was complete, one of the ER docs came to tell us Geoffrey's COVID test came back positive. When the preliminary results from the MRI came out moments later, it thankfully didn't show evidence of a new stroke.

But due to Geoffrey's symptoms and history, he couldn't be discharged. Instead, hours after pulling up at the ER, he would be admitted to the fifth floor and then transferred once more to the third floor, to the unit where both of our boys had bone marrow transplants four years prior.

As we wheeled past the photographs of puffins in the hallway, I felt like I was with old friends. Friends who had stood with me before and were still on the walls for me, today.

There were also nurses who knew us by name, who had seen us at our worst, and loved us still.

I laid down on the pull-out chair beside Geoffrey's bed. He was calm and eating a bowl of Cheerios. It was finally quiet.

I stuck my hand into my pocket to feel the smooth green rock that Mama Micah had given to me that morning—a travel rock, she had said—one for each of us to serve as a reminder that we were loved.

I rubbed the rock between my fingers, a physical reminder of where we were, of a day that looked so different than I could have imagined.

Hope isn't for someday but for this day. It's for the messy, scary middle, before the story has an ending to celebrate or to grieve. Like Emily Dickinson writes:

"Hope" is the thing with feathers -

That perches in the soul -

And sings the tune without the words -

And never stops - at all...[20]

I wanted to say to the little bird within and around me, "Please, don't stop singing. Keep reminding me, and us, that God cares. That we aren't alone."

Geoffrey was three years older than the last time he lived in this hospital space for months. I noticed the ways he was able to verbalize his wants and needs differently now, the ways he processed all of this as a seven-year-

---

20 Emily Dickinson, "Hope is the Thing with Feathers," *The Complete Poems of Emily Dickinson*, edited by Thomas H. Johnson (Boston: Back Bay, 1976).

old. At one point, he pressed the button beside him to call the nursing station, very excited to do it himself.

"How may I help you, Geoffrey," the invisible voice asked.

He giggled as he looked at me and replied, "I need a container, a container to go to the bathroom."

"Your nurse will bring it right in." Geoffrey was delighted by it all.

I texted Baba Micah and Mama Micah again, the exact message I had sent them at least a thousand times before: "Thanks for everything."

Mama Micah responded to reassure me that Ella and Ryan were doing OK. My brother, Uncle Mosh, as we like to call him, was there and had taken Ryan for "chic-e-lay." Ella was calm, watching a show.

"The team back at it," Baba Micah wrote. "These kids are worth every wrinkle!!" And then came a follow-up message: "Your next book should be the story of G. I think he might not be of this world—sent to show us how good we can all be."

* * *

The next morning, the medical team told me they believed Geoffrey had post-stroke recrudescence, a medical term I wasn't familiar with. They explained that his brain was likely inflamed because of COVID and was causing the reappearance of his previously resolved stroke symptoms.

I called Titus to update him, wishing he were here instead of there. And since we didn't know how long we might need to be in LA, my husband and I decided he would make the journey to come be with us.

Geoffrey was discharged after twenty-four hours of observation, and we headed back to the home, family, and community that had lovingly walked with us before and were doing it once again, or maybe *still*. Allowing all of us the time and space needed to rest and heal. Room for both the disappointment of loss and the stubbornness to hope.

Titus and I didn't tell the kids that he was coming, not wanting to create any additional anxiety or disappointments for them if he got stuck along the way. When he arrived, Ella saw him first. "Daddy!" she screamed and ran into his strong and loving arms. Ryan followed right behind her.

Geoffrey, unsteady on his feet, held my hand as we walked toward Titus, his voice echoing loudly through the cool air, "Daddy! Daddy!"

"*Ami yu. Mutyo, mutyo baba, igase?*" I'm here now. I'm sorry. I'm so sorry, do you hear me? I'm here now, Titus assured them all... and me.

Geoffrey needed time to heal, but Daddy's strong and tender presence allowed all of us to exhale. "It's going to be OK. I'm here."

These were the same words Titus spoke four years earlier to Ryan, after horrific complications threatened to steal our little boy. Titus would sit up through the night and hold Ryan on his lap, telling him, "*Ami yu. Ami yu*, Ryan." I am here. I am here.

When Ryan got too sick to be in our arms and a machine was breathing for our boy, he'd repeat the same words still, holding on amid desperation, humming into the darkness. Whispering to his little boy, "I am here."

In our aching and waiting, I can only imagine God's voice lovingly saying the same words to us: I am here. I am here. I am here.

* * *

Henri Nouwen writes, "Amid desperation," we sit, "humming in the darkness," declaring we aren't alone.

Our suffering matters. God is here, closer than you or I know.[21]

By the time a guest arrives at Kimbilio, the doctors have already told them, "There's nothing more we can do." From a curative perspective, that may be true. But as long as there is still breath, there is more to do.

More than treating a disease, at Living Room, we are called to care for a person. A whole person, with a name and a story, who may be asking, "Will I be healed? Will I die? Who will take care of my children? Please make sure my children are OK."

The answers are complex and nuanced, often outside of our control. We ask for life and affirm it in every way we know to do. We come alongside, day and night, caring for the physical, emotional, and spiritual aspects of each man, woman, and child who comes to our doors.

And when they want to know how long it will be, we gently reply, "I don't know."

When will help come? When will the last be first, the wrong be made right? When will I be free from the shame

---

21 Henri Nouwen Society, "Hope means to keep living amid desperation & to keep humming in the darkness," Twitter, February 5, 2021, 7:17 a.m., https://bit.ly/3JKQ6iy.

of my past, of the present, the sickness that plagues my body? When do I need to say good-bye?

Sometimes the questions are asked out loud, sometimes trapped within. Other times still, they present themselves in unexpected ways.

One Wednesday morning, as I did rounds with our clinical team at Kimbilio, a woman named Veronica was experiencing anxiety as she approached her final days, an aggressive cancer filling much of her body.

We had been able to get her pain and other symptoms controlled, but she complained of feeling anxious. I asked her if she wanted medicine to help her to relax. Without acknowledging my question, she replied, *"Tuimbe."* Let's sing.

Veronica began to lead a hymn in Swahili, *"Chakutumaini sina ila damu yake Yesu."* My hope is built on nothing less than Jesus' blood and righteousness. The others in the room joined in her singing.

The hope in her song wasn't linked to a happy ending to her hard story. We would have gladly welcomed healing to come through a cure for her cancer, but there must be enough room within our hope for suffering and loss, for sorrow and lament.

Lament, as Cole Arthur Riley writes, "is an innate awareness that what is should not be. As if something is written on our hearts that tells us exactly what we are meant for, and whenever confronted with something contrary to this, we experience a crumbling. And in the rubble, we say, God, you promised. We ask, why? And how could we experience such devastation if we were not on some mysterious plane, hoping for something different? Our hope can be only as deep as our lament is. And our lament as deep as our hope." [22]

Hope allows us to weep with those who weep, to wait and ache with the expectation that all that is wrong will one day soon be made right.

Until then, I'll keep humming in the darkness.

---

22 Cole Arthur Riley, *This Here Flesh: Spirituality, Liberation, and the Stories That Make Us* (New York: Convergent, 2022), 101.

I find it a surprise
how often joy and sadness,
refusing to take turns,
overlap.
More than sitting side by side,
it's hard to distinguish
where one begins and the other ends.
Perhaps neither can be
fully awake and alive
without enough room for the other.

Chapter Twelve

Joy and Sadness

Ryan came to our home as a two-week-old baby weighing three pounds. Every two hours, I fed him a teaspoon of formula. I swaddled him and rocked back and forth, feeling the sadness and loss of the mother who was supposed to still have him in her body, the mother who tragically died while bringing her son into the world.

I don't know what happened to her that night in April of 2016. Her body was brought to Kimbilio Funeral Home the next morning.

I held baby Ryan and grieved for a mother whom I would only come to know through the wonder of her little ones. I held a baby and hummed in the night as I rocked him back and forth and prayed that the joy of God would always be Ryan's strength. Not sure what that meant, it was the constant prayer that arose from within me.

I knew that my love didn't remove his loss.

When Ryan was six months old, the unexpected pain of sickle cell made its way into his toes and then his thumb and moved from place to place on any given day. I ached deeply and continued to pray for relief while also longing for life and joy to be his.

* * *

Throughout my journey of living in Kenya, one of the things I've experienced in being near to suffering is that joy and sadness can coexist. In hospice work, the expectation is that there will be sadness and pain, rather than the combination we often see. But, at times, there are also people who come with deep depression and total pain that make joy more elusive.

Joy isn't something we can always choose and cling to. It is a mysterious gift from God that can be found in the midst of sadness, just as sadness can accompany joy.

As I've heard it said before, mourning and dancing don't always take turns.

Since early 2011, our Living Room team has had the privilege to care for a girl named Grace who has cerebral palsy. On the night she first arrived at Kimbilio Hospice, she was on the verge of starvation, an eight-year-old weighing a mere thirteen pounds.

Our community-based team had been called to come and check on her and found her locked and alone in a house. Her condition seemed incompatible with life.

The day she was admitted, our small team of caregivers at Kimbilio gently held Grace's broken body, feeding her, ever so slowly, a milk-based formula.

On the second day she was with us, I watched as Mary, one of Living Room's caregivers, held Grace on her lap and sang a hymn in Kalenjin: *"Abaibai amu chama Jeso, chama Jeso mising."* I am so glad that Jesus loves me, Jesus loves even me.

As she sang, a smile as beautiful as it was surprising filled Grace's face. Everyone in the room was overcome with wonder. Mary just kept singing of love, and Grace began to laugh in a way I hope to never forget.

I find encouragement in these words by Henri Nouwen, "Be surprised by joy, be surprised by the little flower that shows its beauty in the midst of a barren desert and be surprised by the immense healing power that keeps bursting forth like springs for fresh water from the depth of our pain."[23]

Day by day, as love was poured into Grace, she grew and became a part of us. Even though Kimbilio wasn't

---

23 Henri Nouwen, *You Are the Beloved: Daily Meditations for Spiritual Living* (New York: Convergent Books, 2017), 94.

intended to be a long-term care facility, Grace has needed a place to stay that would protect and nurture her.

We've looked at taking her back to the community to be with family, and we enrolled her in a special needs school, but neither has been good nor safe for her. So, she stays with us.

I find the experience of joy so difficult to describe. It transcends spoken language. Maybe this is partly why Grace, in so many ways, has been my greatest teacher in it. Though unable to speak, she isn't limited by human language.

It isn't that Grace doesn't have days filled with sadness and crying. She is a beautifully complex human being, and like the rest of us, she feels pain and sorrow and frustration.

On so many days, though, if you were to visit Living Room's Kimbilio Hospice, you would find Grace sitting on the veranda or in the garden. She would greet you with her radiant smile and the uncontrolled, nonverbal sounds which are generous and filled with meaning, if you are willing to listen. They rise from a place deep within her. No matter your singing ability, if you sing to her, she will laugh and try to sing with you, too.

When I think about joy, moments spent with my friend Grace are what resonate within me. Moments that are fleeting and catch me off guard, nearly taking my breath away. They often bring tears to my eyes, warranting my full attention, leaving me unsure of what just happened, all the while, filled with wonder.

Once, while visiting a children's hospital on the other side of the world, I was invited to share insights about caring for medically fragile children like Grace. I met a little boy whose name I do not know and whom I will likely never meet again. On a day when I needed to be reminded of love, I leaned down to greet him, and he hugged me and wouldn't let go.

Like Grace, he wasn't verbal, but as a friend of mine says, his silence was a language—a language I wasn't prepared for, the way his unrestrained love ministered to me. But I leaned in, soaking in the gift of his embrace, experiencing what Jan Richardson rightly captures:

...it will astonish you

how wide your heart

will open

in welcome

for the joy

that finds you

so ready

and still so

unprepared.[24]

* * *

Just prior to our move back to Kenya after our boys' treatment, I heard a word in the night. It wasn't audible, but it was clear, surprising, and imprinted within my spirit when I woke up the next morning. *Enjoy.* I recognized it as an invitation to slow down and notice, to not miss the healing, slow as molasses, that was finally coming for our little boys.

The night had long stayed pitch black and scary, but death didn't win this time. The traumas of treatment were evident within and all around. My nervous system had been pushed beyond its limits. Silent prayers were all I had to pray, but they were still prayers. And they were heard. As worn out as I was—physically, emotionally, spiritually—I welcomed the possibility of joy and delight.

Once we got home to Kenya, I waxed and waned between a state of shutting down to having flashbacks of an ICU where scary machines beeped and rattled

---

24 Jan Richardson, "Advent 4: For Joy," The Advent Door: Entering A Contemplative Christmas, December 20, 2012, https://bit. ly/3JKKx3I.

constantly. A place where breathing stopped and tears flowed.

Experiencing Geoffrey's treatment journey only a few months after Ryan's was like long COVID—it just kept going and going and felt like it might not ever end. It might not get better.

For months, a dig-deep sort of perseverance and grit were required for the cyclical pattern of Geoffrey getting a little better and then having another complication that would knock him, and us, further down.

Even though the boys were now doing well, I no longer knew how to judge when an illness might be serious or just a common cold. Everything had been flashing and blaring for so long, like a fire alarm—danger, danger, danger. Now, I didn't know how to turn it off.

A few months after we returned, Ryan developed a fast-spreading infection in his right big toe. I sent a photo on a Saturday evening to our pediatrician in Eldoret. She wrote back that she was consulting with a surgeon and infectious disease doctor to see what we should do next.

By Sunday morning, we were meeting with three specialists, trying to come up with a plan, uncertain of what was causing the swelling, redness, and necrotic tissue on my baby's toe.

My body held the memory of all the days and nights Ryan was sick and in the hospital. Sometimes, the memory was tucked away neatly. Other times, a trigger came uninvited, unannounced, and it transported me back to a moment when death was too close, too scary.

After much consultation, we also met with an entomologist. (We are incredibly blessed to have remarkable friends in all these areas of specialty to help when needed!) Our friend, Dino, was convinced Ryan had been bitten by a spider and would recover.

As we were driving home from seeing the doctors, a song about the goodness of God came on. When the song ended, Ryan, then barely three but still only speaking a few words, said, "Again!"

It surprised me, as I had never heard him say that word before. I turned to look at Ryan in his car seat, tears in my eyes.

"Again?" I asked.

This little one, who had survived so very much, gave a hearty, "Yes!"

We listened again, and I took a deep breath and let the words soak in. To be invited to feel joy isn't a matter of shaming the unhealed parts of our trauma that need loving patience. There is room for the slow work of healing and joy to coexist, sitting side by side and holding hands.

Motherhood has left stretch marks across my body and soul. I regularly meet with a counselor and spiritual director to notice and talk about it, or sometimes to be still and listen.

What I hear is that the trauma of motherhood that has wounded me hasn't canceled—not for a moment— the joy of motherhood, or the goodness and mercy of God. It continues to run after me.

* * *

These days, I keep finding my way outside, morning after morning, and throughout the day, to look at the sky and the trees, to listen to the birds, to feel the solid ground beneath my feet.

One morning, at Geoffrey's request, I rode my bike on the uneven dirt paths, following behind four of our kids. Alice didn't feel like riding that day and stayed at home, but the rest of the crew climbed on their bikes and started down the road.

Sharon and Ella took turns leading, and Ryan pedaled vigorously to stay close to the front. Geoffrey pedaled by my side, laughing with delight as he drove through a puddle. He loved doing this together. I did too. Balance isn't easy for him, but he has worked hard to learn to ride a bike. He pushed the right pedal with his braced foot and said a phrase he has repeated since he was little: "Mama, you know we can do hard things!"

"Yes, we can, Geoffrey!"

I was reminded of our transplant days when he used a blue, yellow, and red tricycle and his imagination to explore the great unknown while trapped in a hospital room. Like today, even then, he was inviting me along on his adventure.

One day, while in the hospital, Geoffrey needed to leave his room to go for an ultrasound. But when the transport man arrived with his stretcher, Geoffrey didn't want to get on it. He asked if he could ride his bike instead. He was surprisingly permitted, and off he went in his blue and red fire truck pajamas, a triceratops riding in the yellow basket behind him.

"You're the first one I've taken like this," the kind transport man told Geoffrey.

Geoffrey pedaled down the long hallway to the elevator, his face puffy beyond recognition from all the steroids, his voice filled with joy. "I'm racing you! I'm racing you!"

"I'm racing you," the transport man replied, laughing back to him. "I can't catch you!"

"Phew, we made it!" Geoffrey said as we arrived at the elevator doors.

Joy overflowing.

* * *

It feels important to recognize that sadness isn't the opposite of joy. Fear is.

And while there must be grace and tenderness for each of us to find our way through the scary mess, we cannot stay there.

I want joy to still be possible. I want to love with courage, knowing that courage requires vulnerability. Like Brené Brown writes, "No emotion is more frightening than joy, because we believe if we allow ourselves to feel joy, we are inviting disaster... But there's a huge cost (to foreboding joy). When we push away joy, we squander the goodness that we need to build resilience, strength, and courage."[25]

I go outside on many a day to find two brothers climbing a mango tree together, just as it should be. I stand at a distance, but close enough to listen to their

---

25 Brené Brown, *Atlas of the Heart: Mapping Meaningful Connection and the Language of Human Experience* (New York: Random House, 2022), 216.

tales and to the sound of their exuberant laughter. I'm grateful, deeply grateful, they have one another.

There is a pang of joy I feel and ponder it all in my heart. A road marked with great loss and suffering and healing is only a piece of their story. There is also wonder and play and love that is deep and wide and holds us all together. I want to lean in and enjoy.

* * *

One early morning not long ago, Ella ran into our room, thrilled by the brilliant blue and red turacos in our trees. Capturing the moment, her small voice directed at me: "Mom, this is the bird you have been waiting to see." It made me think of these joy-filled words by Mary Oliver:[26]

Oh do you have time

to linger

for just a little while

out of your busy

and very important day

for the goldfinches

---

26 Mary Oliver, "Invitation," *Red Bird* (Boston: Beacon Press, 2009), 18.

that have gathered...

for sheer delight and gratitude—

believe us, they say,

it is a serious thing

just to be alive

on this fresh morning

in the broken world.

* * *

When I began to write what would become *From Beyond the Skies,* I didn't see it as an exercise in gratitude. Looking back, though, that's very much what it was. A long exercise in sitting down to remember, to notice and name. To hold onto what is good even when hard things remain.

It started while we were in the middle of the treatment, before there was anything like an outcome to celebrate. The process was raw and didn't leave room for wishful thinking or an attempt to create a reason, or extra meaning, for the hard and horrible things that were happening to us and around us. No toxic positivity to cancel my sadness or ignore the pain.

For the words that came after we arrived back in Kenya, I was able to go back, with my mind and my body, to look at the hard, but to also see goodness. Then, I tried to leave room for words to describe it. It was my way to simultaneously grieve and to begin to say thank you. Not for diagnoses or my children's needless suffering—I don't feel the need to give those my gratitude. But for the goodness and mercy that accompanied us, I'll ever be grateful.

With uncertainty, I leaned in and found room to feel and process. I didn't show a word of the writing to anyone until I had written the messy first draft. Fifty thousand words of unfiltered, imperfect, received prayers.

The themes of goodness and love within community, of kindness found, came up over and over again. My thanks wrapped around the world, filling an entire book.

My ninety-six-year-old grandma, Granny Bettie, was the first person to read the book when I received the printed copies. She read it in a day and generously wrote: "This is a story of our loving God and his mysterious ways!"

When the book was released, our family returned in person to say thank you to the people and places in Kenya and Los Angeles who had accompanied us. We gave *From Beyond the Skies* to the doctors at the hospital in Eldoret, to our staff at Living Room, as well as to some of our neighbors, to our doctors, nurses, and team at UCLA, to our church family, to the Herberts, and to so many friends, all over the world.

Perhaps we all need to remember how to slow down, enjoy, and insist on saying thank you. To remember the kindness of many, allowing the joy and the sadness of a remarkable journey to have enough room.

Like an unrelenting mother,

God loves us.

In tangible and tender ways.

Unable to forget.

Unwilling to give up.

Ready to go to any length.

And to anywhere.

All for the sake of love.

Chapter Thirteen

A Mother's Love

I dreamt of becoming a mother for many years, longing to have a child and family of my own. I know it's not everyone's dream, but it was mine. At thirty-three years old, five months after marrying Titus, I developed an unrelenting craving for oranges, and the pregnancy test confirmed, to our great joy, that we were going to have a baby.

A few weeks later, at my first prenatal visit in Eldoret, I read a sign on my obstetrician's desk: "A child gives birth to a mother." Before becoming a mother, I had always thought of labor only in reference to birthing a child, instead of it also being required to become a mother. I hadn't yet considered that the laboring into motherhood may never end.

On a rainy, cold night, the last day of July, I held Ella for the first time. Her tiny hand wrapped around my finger as her beautiful brown eyes met mine. She rested her face against my chest. This baby girl had made me a mother, and I was overwhelmed with joy, delighted and relieved that she was finally here.

But there was also a piece of me that understood it would be harder to protect her now that she was no longer housed within my body. The cord that connected me to her, the shelter that made room for her to grow and nurtured her in all the ways she needed, was no longer available to her or to me.

I knew motherhood was going to teach me to love in a new way, but I didn't comprehend how messy and scary, how uncontrollable, it would all feel. My body, like those of all new mamas, was exhausted from pregnancy and labor. I hurt in places I had never felt before. I wanted to be alert and present to every moment, to feel joy and gratitude, but I also wanted to sleep. I wanted to take a shower. To go to the bathroom. To eat. To take a walk. To read a book.

All those things, suddenly, were elusive.

I like to say that I was an excellent mom before I had a child, when parenting was only theoretical. When my baby slept through the night, every night, in her own crib. When I was calm and responded appropriately in stressful situations, even when exhausted and hungry.

When breastfeeding was natural and painless. When I was patient and kind and knew what to do and how to do it, and my baby was consolable.

I had never felt so vulnerable as I did during Ella's newborn phase. I was lonely while never actually being alone. What I had known in my head about being a mom from all the books I read wasn't going to be enough.

I needed community to support me as I learned to mother my baby. It was my time and my turn, in my own unique way, to become a mother.

* * *

On a Wednesday afternoon, long before I had my babies, a young mother arrived at Kimbilio Hospice in search of help. Her five-year-old son's face, grossly disfigured by a massive tumor, explained the reason for her coming, her desperation.

She, like any mother, was willing to do anything within her means to save the life of her child. Unfortunately, like so many around the world, she had limited means. She lived in a land where the early detection and treatment of cancer are rare, and where suffering is too often in plenty. This mother told us a story of her futile attempts to get treatment for her little boy, Masese.

Until a few months earlier, her son had been healthy. A small wound had appeared on the left side of his face, but when it failed to heal and continued to grow, she took him to the local hospital. The doctor sent her home without a proper diagnosis or any treatment plan.

In the hopes of saving her child, she traveled seven hours on a *matatu,* a private minibus used as a shared taxi, to see an herbalist that lives near Kipkaren.

With one look at the child, the herbalist told the mother there was nothing he could do for them. She was devastated, and not knowing what to do next, she climbed on the back of a *pikipiki,* a motorbike taxi, with her little boy. The driver told her that she should go to Kimbilio. "It's the place where people are helped," he told her.

She agreed to come, and he drove them to us.

As I sat with this mama and listened to her story, I imagined the days and nights that she cried out to God for help. As I listened to her that day, I had no way of knowing that, one day, I would pray those same types of prayers, desperate and longing for God to move on behalf of my children.

* * *

Before I became a mother, I was a nurse and global health advocate (and apparently a *yaya*). For over a decade, I cared about the suffering of others. I listened and learned and walked alongside. I held the hands of many a person, and I bandaged many wounds.

I've witnessed the fierce, unbridled love of motherhood reach as deep as it does wide. I've seen a mother carry her thirty-year-old daughter on her back, walking to an HIV clinic, trying to get her the treatment she needed. She leaned forward with every step, balancing her daughter's weight and length on her own body.

I've watched a young, gravely ill mother arrive at Kimbilio Hospice, her body wasted from disease, not able to eat for nearly two days. As we examined her, she attempted to offer her breast to her six-month-old little girl, a child who weighed a mere five pounds.

I've stood at the bedside of many a mother as she prepares to die, when she's asked, "What do you need today?" The same request is spoken again and again: "Please promise me that my children will be OK."

Like these holy, catch-your-breath moments that have demonstrated for me the love and sacrifice of mothers, poet Joel Leon writes of his own mother's love and captures the meaning in it for us:

I never watched my mother

walk on water but

I saw her wait for the bus

in the snow to pay the rent

we define holy differently.[27]

Witnessing the love of other mothers in these hard and sacred moments planted seeds within me that would one day grow when my turn came to mother my children.

Motherhood reshaped me on a deeper level than anything I had known before, especially when my own children were diagnosed with sickle cell disease.

In 2016, when Ryan was barely six months old, our lives and family already looked so different than we had imagined. His unexpected presence in our home, our adoption journey, his siblings—those were our storylines.

Added to that was the grief of his parents' untimely deaths, as well as the fragility and joy of Ryan's unlikely survival as a premature baby, born with complications in a rural home birth. Ryan's story already had enough loss, struggle, and complexity. I thought we were to the

27 Joel Leon, "i never saw my mother walk on water but i saw her wait for the bus in the snow to pay the rent we define holy differently," Twitter, December 30, 2019, 3:24 p.m., https://bit.ly/3JKKUv8.

redemption part of the story, where he'd already been welcomed into a home with a family that loved him so much.

That was enough. Then one dark night, out of nowhere, came the ferocious pain in his feet, his unfamiliar cries from a source none of us recognized. Within a week, pathology results came by email. A PDF held the devastating news that Ryan had sickle cell disease.

I felt the heaviness of his diagnosis, combined with how dramatically our location affected his prognosis. In the US, the life expectancy for a person living with sickle cell disease was forty-two years. While that isn't good, it was very different from the five-year life expectancy in Kenya.

It wasn't just about the threat of death but also the amounts of suffering and the ways his life would be marked by pain that I knew was coming and was already here.

Within weeks, we'd have diagnoses for Geoffrey and Alice, too. Ella was still a toddler, needing plenty of her mama's time and attention. All of it was overwhelming during good moments, crushing the rest of the time.

* * *

Some two years later, I was back in Kenya, and a shift occurred in the lens through which I saw patient care. The shift followed the unbelievable journey of our boys having transplants that led to their cures, after all the days and nights living in the hospital, the IV lines, the beeping of machines, the traumas of treatment, the complications that led us to the razor's edge of death, the healing that would not, could not, be hurried.

I couldn't separate the nurse and clinical director from the mother within me who had just lived fifteen months in and out of the hospital.

At first, I simply felt the shift. I didn't have words for it, didn't speak of it much. I thought I would adjust back to the clinical, professional self, separate from the mother. But in meetings or interactions with our hospital spaces, or patients and their families, I kept advocating as a mother, with words, decisions, planning, and interactions.

It's not that I didn't have boundaries or understand my role and position, but now I asked questions that seemed important to know and understand.

Why aren't there more hospitals in Kenya that train their nurses in pediatrics? Where are mothers and children who've traveled far for their treatment supposed to stay? Why should children die of a treatable disease, and what can we do about it? How can we reduce the suffering for the children who come into our care? How do we make a hospital less scary, more welcoming, for children and parents?

* * *

There's an African proverb that says, "When you pray, move your feet."

I recognize there is immense value to being still in prayer, to listening, and seasons when waiting is what is being asked of us. But as this proverb infers, prayer also involves response and action. It is much like love.

Love is more than words spoken from our mouths. It must be lived out in the patterns and actions of our lives. The urgency of "doing justly" and "loving mercy" sometimes looks like climbing on a bus for seven hours, unsure of what will be on the other side of the ride (see Mic. 6:8).

It's in the giving of the last drops of milk in your breast, knowing it isn't enough, but it's all you have to give. It's in making room to open our doors wide, in the asking of questions that might make a hard journey a little less so for others.

It's in advocating with the belief that, even if a mother could forget, God will not.

* * *

Kimbilio exists to serve the poor and the otherwise neglected. Because of this, we often attract cases that, when seen with human eyes, seem beyond hope. Maybe it shouldn't surprise me, but time and again, it does: love and intensive care—physical, emotional, and spiritual— often give way to what feels like miracles.

One of the tragedies accompanying the AIDS pandemic in Africa is that children have too often been reduced to "burdens of society."

On the day several months ago that a baby named Chepkemboi was admitted to Kimbilio Hospice, she was terribly sick with the same virus that would shortly take the life of her mother. For nine months, they had been tied together. Chepkemboi's mother had labored for the sake of her child and cared for her, although both of their bodies were ailing. At Kimbilio, mother and baby shared a bed, until, one day, the mother was no more.

Chepkemboi's tiny body was emaciated, weakened by poor nutrition and the effects of being HIV positive. She needed intensive care, and for a season, the Living Room team became her family.

Over the past months, we have fed and bathed, clothed and loved, this *mtoto*, this child. We have stepped into a gap that deserved to be filled. As a result, we have anticipated and celebrated Chepkemboi's first steps.

Like all children, her first words were *mama* and *baba*, but in her case, there are numerous mothers and fathers providing her care. She has imitated the pattern of some other little ones to carry on the practice of calling me *yaya*.

This week, Chepkemboi will turn two. In her honor, we are hosting a birthday party. As Chepkemboi's *mamas, babas,* and *yaya*, we will get to sing and dance, share a cake, and thank God for the life of this little girl.

* * *

When we love, broken things of this world are restored and made new—even if, sometimes, it is in death.

For Masese, we watched what felt like a miracle, as the tumor on his face shrunk and slowly disappeared under the treatment of chemotherapy. Alongside his mama, we were so grateful and amazed by the recovery that took place.

Some four months later, with incredible speed and aggression, the tumor regrew and disfigured Masese's face once more. A new diagnosis was given, and a new treatment plan developed.

We would raise funds and travel far and wide to get Masese the radiation therapy he needed. When the treatment failed, we cared for him still, treating his pain and making space in the hospice for him to rest.

At Living Room, we have long held and attempted to live out the value of accompaniment, of walking alongside our patients and their families. We did this with Masese and his mother—in his sickness, in death, in grief.

I don't have the answers to why some children heal and others die. Most days, it feels like even if there were an answer to such untellable loss and grief, asking why wouldn't be helpful. What I care about more is knowing that God is close to the hurting, to the suffering, to the brokenhearted.

I need my heart to make room for the messiness of grief, to trust that the way we love matters. I never underestimate, though, what every mother knows: how hard it is to love. It is costly and requires vulnerability, but I am convinced that, like motherhood itself, it is worth it.

It is worth breathing deep and leaning in, even on nights I am tired, yet asked by little voices to read one more book. To get one more cup of water to quench a thirst. To sing one more song—Ella negotiating for two. To pray one more prayer.

The mosquito nets get tucked in tightly, and then one or all need to go to the bathroom again, and we start the process over. One more time.

In our family's journey, there are also days when I hear Ryan say from the other room, "Me miss my other mom and my other dad. What happened to them, anyway?"

On nights like those, Geoffrey is quiet as Ella tries to explain the situation. "Your mom died when you were born," she says in the way she understands it.

"Oh, that makes me sad," Ryan says every time.

On nights like those, I go into the room and leave space for his sadness. I am his mom, and he and his other siblings have lost their mother to death. I am not her replacement.

There is enough room for their loss and grief, both present and what may come. And there is enough room for my love.

"I love you, Ryan."

"Me loves you, too."

Mama Micah and I often text each other, in various forms, only sort of kidding: "Love is patient, and love is kind. But do we have to do both, at the same time?! I mean, it feels like it is asking a lot."

To be clear, it is.

* * *

"Mama, what's God doing?" Ryan asked out of the blue one morning while I buttered his toast.

Unsure of what he meant, I repeated his question back to him. "Ryan, what do *you* think God's doing?"

"He's loving us," he replied, as he continued to build his tower of dominoes.

I paused to hold the sacred of an ordinary moment. To tuck Ryan's words away inside the treasure chest of my heart. To look him in the eye and affirm his wisdom. "I believe it, too, Ryan."

This love Ryan was talking about is for us to notice, to receive, to extend. To find ourselves unconditionally loved.

Nothing in all the world has taught me the depths of love like being a mother.

For those living in a world,
inside a body overflowing with unrelieved pain.
With hopes that feel dangerous
and fears that seem reasonable.
For those who hold the trauma
of unseeable suffering that
hasn't always been believed or treated with care.
May you know your worth—
and be embraced by ones who do justly and love
mercifully.

Chapter Fourteen

Sickle Cell

Months after we had completed the boys' transplants, I came across a watercolor painting on Etsy—an abstract print of plump red, orange, and yellow circles, depicting healthy red and white blood cells. Tears welled up from some place deep within, surprising me with awe and wonder. Healthy blood cells just like these, once a world away, now fill our little boys.

I ordered the print and wrote a message to the artist, thanking her for her work and asking if she would consider painting another print of sickled cells. She agreed and created a combination of round and crescent-moon-shaped cells in shades of red, yellow, and purple, a depiction of the histology of sickle cell anemia.

I hung the prints in my kitchen, a reminder of what once was in our sons, and what still is within Alice and so many other children in Western Kenya.

Six years ago, these abstract paintings would have had no meaning to me. Now, they represent the unlikely journey we have found ourselves on as a family.

I first entered this journey as a mother, but more and more, as time goes by, and my heart and mind have capacity, I find my role as a nurse to advocate for other patients and families, too.

In the painter's abstract style, as in our journey, there are elements of before, after, and elements of still. Questions of how, what if, and why not.

* * *

Titus, Alice, Sharon, and I sat around our kitchen table a few weeks after returning to Kenya. Yet again, we had the impossible conversation of why Alice's two little brothers traveled across the world for treatment that ultimately cured them of their sickle cell disease, and why she didn't get to go. Of how she didn't have a donor match to undergo bone marrow transplant, but they did. Of why her body still pains every day, while her brothers have begun to forget how much they once hurt.

We talked about the reasons she goes to the clinic and has labs drawn, why she takes medication each day and needs to avoid triggers like heat and cold, dehydration, stress, and basically everything else under the sun.

In Kenya, it is estimated that up to 90 percent of children with sickle cell disease die before they turn five. Alice is thirteen years old, and while we are grateful that she has long outlived her life expectancy, it doesn't feel like enough.

We want more life. More hope. More healing.

Alice is kindhearted and thoughtful. She works hard and excels in school and loves to eat mangoes and to crochet hats with a flower on the front for her brother. She likes to have her hair braided with long extensions and to wear a flowing dress made of kitenge material. She's quiet and giggles often, and she's stubborn if you try to slow her down, even if it's for her own protection.

Alice is so much more than a diagnosis to fix or treat, more complex than the anemia that often leaves her tired and threatens her organs. And she's more than the prognosis associated with children living with sickle cell disease in Kenya. She is so much more.

Alice rarely complains about her pain, but when you'd ask how often it hurts, she'd tell you, *"Kila siku."* Every day.

"Wapi?" Where?

"Mostly my legs. Sometimes my back."

Until her littlest brother Ryan was born and got his diagnosis at nearly six months old, no one understood why Alice so often hurt to the point of screaming in anguish. Why their brother who died at the age of two also hurt. Why Geoffrey so often hurt.

There was talk in the community of them being cursed. They'd go to a clinic and get treated for malaria, but the unpredictable, excruciating pain always came back. I wish I, or anyone else, for that matter, could have told their mama, "Your beautiful babies aren't cursed. They're sick and need medicine."

It wouldn't have erased their disease or fixed their pain, but perhaps the naming could have given her more power and access to help and hope.

* * *

There are major challenges for children affected by sickle cell disease in Kenya. There isn't routine newborn screening, and many don't survive to get a proper diagnosis.

And since most live in rural communities, they're too far from the larger, better equipped hospitals that would at least give them a chance to have their disease monitored and treated. To take the prophylactic penicillin and get immunizations to reduce their high risk of bacterial infections and sepsis. To take preventative medicine to reduce their chance of getting malaria. To start early on hydroxyurea to reduce some of the pain crises and other complications. To give them more of the support and care required for them to have a chance to survive.

* * *

After returning to Kenya, there were many aspects of patient care that I did not return to, as my administrative responsibilities in opening Living Room's hospital kept me more than busy. Certain parts of care, though, especially with pediatric patients affected by sickle cell disease, were constantly on my mind and heart. Somewhere in the middle of the pandemic, I started asking questions about sickle cell disease in Western Kenya that I hadn't had the capacity until then to ask.

For a season, I needed space to compartmentalize the sickness of my children from the much bigger picture that impacts this region. More and more, though, I wanted to understand both the disease and the lived experience within this context, recognizing that everyone's story is uniquely their own.

I was familiar with the high volume of children living with sickle cell disease in the area, as a doctor I knew had told me over lunch one day. That they treated more than two hundred children with sickle cell disease in their outpatient clinic.

"By the time these children are supposed to transition to the adolescent clinic, none are still alive," he lamented.

His words haunted me and led to many more conversations about what could be done to improve outcomes.

I was glad to get a call, one afternoon, from a pediatrician starting a sickle cell clinic at a hospital just twenty miles or so from Kipkaren. "I was told you're good at sickle cell," she told me after introducing herself. "I wanted to see if we could meet and see if there are opportunities to partner."

"Good at sickle cell" isn't likely the best way to describe my connection to the disease. Twenty years ago, I took care of adult patients with sickle cell while working in a hospital in Los Angeles. And for the past six years, I've been immersed in it as a mother—times three.

From the love of my kids, I have become passionate about understanding more about the pathophysiology, the complications, and the treatment options available here as compared to the States. To try and to connect with other providers and parents in Kenya to learn more about what is currently available within practice and what the next steps might be.

As a nurse who has long worked in community health and has lived in a rural village for eighteen years, I've contemplated the determinants of health beyond medical treatment alone that play such a large role in both survival and quality of life.

"I'm not sure I'm *good* at sickle cell," I told her, "but I care very much and would love to meet you."

That phone call led to a series of meetings and further conversations about working together to implement first steps that may appear small, but only time will tell their significance. These steps include listening to the experiences and stories of other mothers, learning about the barriers that keep them from getting the care their child needs, making room for their voices to be augmented, empowering them through education, and advocating for resources to improve their care.

I look back on the last six years of being a mama to three children with sickle cell disease and understand that I have had a plethora of resources and opportunities available to me that most fellow Kenyans do not have.

From medical knowledge and connections, to travel ability.

From insurance that would pay for treatment, to years of experience of advocating for other patients.

From things as simple as food, clean water, and mosquito nets, to transportation availability when one or more of our kids needed to be rushed to the hospital.

From job stability, to access to morphine because we run a hospice.

From a strong network of friends and family who have loved and supported us, to accessing treatment that led to a cure that isn't yet existing in Kenya.

And even with all of these resources available to me, the journey has been longer, harder, and scarier than anything I have ever known. There have been nights in the hospital when I've wondered if we'd make it to the morning, but at least we had access to a hospital.

As a result, I'm constantly asking, wondering, and praying: *How can more of this be available to others too?*

* * *

Before the launch of *From Beyond the Skies,* I made a paper chain with my kids. On the twelve days leading up to the launch, we removed one link each day until book release day.

Making paper chains like this is a family tradition. As a child, I loved counting down the days leading up to Christmas, removing a green or red construction paper link each day.

When Ryan's transplant journey began, I am not sure what made me decide to create a paper link chain, adding a link each day, but that's what I did. It all went well until, somewhere in the middle of the treatment, when we got way too close to death, I wanted to give up on the paper chain. My mom told me I couldn't quit.

A chain with sixty-one paper links filled Ryan's windowsill on the day we were finally told he could go home. I didn't imagine I'd ever make a paper chain again.

When it came to the book launch, though, Geoffrey and Ryan were excited to take off a link every day until our book was released into the world.

As feedback started to flood my inbox, I was so moved, and not just by people's reactions to our story or to my writing. I was grateful for the encouragement and positive reviews, but it was the many requests and comments about practical ways to respond that I found most moving.

One friend wrote that when she finished reading the book, she went to donate blood and platelets.

Others shared they signed up for the registry to be potential donors for Be the Match.

A nurse who works in a transplant unit wrote to say, "I feel like I understand my work so much better because of your words."

Another nurse shared, "Reading your amazing book in my hospice nurse scrubs waiting for the next call..."

One doctor told me that after reading the book, he listens to his patients with sickle cell differently. He said that he goes a little slower, takes more time in the way that he listens and treats them.

All of it felt surprising and loving and kind.

We all have stories to tell of the ways we've been shaped by pain and forced, in a sense, to become "good" at a hard thing, simply because someone we love is impacted by it. We have learned the profound experience of being "bound by a common anguish," to use Harper Lee's words.[28]

Shared suffering, while unique to each one's lived experience, allows one mama to say to another, in the middle of the hard, "Oh, you get it. You get it!"

---

28 Casey Cep, "Why Harper Lee Struggled to Write a Book After *To Kill a Mockingbird,*" *Time*, May 7, 2019, https://bit.ly/43aaQHk.

Reaching out to others who have experienced a similar kind of pain, offering what insight and knowledge we've gained, is one of the ways love makes us brave.

Maybe death has lost its sting,
and comfort is the promised blessing
for the sadness, the angst of mourning.
Grief is not in a hurry, though,
and follows its own set of rules.
Thankfully, love is patient and kind.
It always protects, always trusts,
always hopes, always perseveres.

Chapter Fifteen

Grief

A large, gray-brownish bird with iridescent gloss on its wings lives in our community. It's called a hadada ibis. Everything about it looks prehistoric to me, so I call it a dinosaur bird.

Ella has her own name for it, referring to it as "the fussy bird." Hadadas don't sing a pretty song; they have a loud, disturbing "ha-da-da" call. Uncomfortable to be around and to listen to as it screams uninhibited into the sky, the call of the hadada has come to represent lament to me.

I hear it asking, "How long?" and "Why?" and have grown tender toward these questions of its cries.

I am a mother to children who have already witnessed the death and burial of their parents. Sometimes, the weight of grief unexpectedly falls heavily on our kids, and we make room for the unfiltered messiness of it.

Space for unanswerable questions to be whispered or shouted.

As a mom, I don't always recognize that this is what is happening in the moment. I can confuse their grief with a bad attitude or laziness. It's usually not that straightforward, and yet I long to be patient and kind with them, to listen well, even when words aren't available to them or to me.

I think of Jesus standing outside a tomb where his friend's body is buried, knowing his voice holds the power to call him back from death. In a story that could easily be focused on victory, Jesus cried (see John 11:32–44). Was he overwhelmed by sorrow or anger, or both? Do we really need to know why, or can we leave room for a God who cries too?

* * *

I recently received an unexpected Facebook message from the brother of a patient I helped care for sixteen years ago. His message was brief but tender. His brother Kiptoo was just twelve when he died of advanced heart failure, and this younger brother wrote to say thank you, all these years later.

He shared of remembering how important our team was to his family when his brother was sick, and how his brother often called for me in his dreams, something I'd not known before. He said we had brought hope during really hard times.

The morning Kiptoo died, we went to be with the family to say, *"Pole."* I'm sorry for your loss. Some collected firewood to cook food for the family and neighbors gathering for the burial. Others sifted a pot of beans to remove stray pebbles. Still others simply sat on a hillside, the hill with a view that extended far and wide, providing beauty on a day when our little part of the world felt sad.

By the time I met Kiptoo, he was already very sick. We took him to the hospital for medical workups and got him the care that was available at the time, which was less than the care he needed.

Kiptoo had a quiet voice, but when he spoke, we listened. He advocated for himself until he knew he could trust us to do it for him. We sure tried.

His stick-thin limbs and grossly distended belly told a story of the extent of his disease, but it didn't capture the light of his smile or the wonder of his mind. Often, when we'd stop by his home, he would be rewiring an old radio, trying to get extra juice out of the used batteries in the hope of listening to the grainy sound of a gospel song in Swahili.

On the day I received the Facebook message, I recalled the morning all those years ago when Kiptoo had died and I stood beside his mother, tears in our eyes. Kiptoo's body lay on a mattress on the floor. His mama told me of how he and his little brother slept side by side on that mattress. How Kiptoo's little brother didn't know he was dead until that morning and kept asking him to scoot over.

Preparations were made for Kiptoo's body to be placed in the ground that same day—a rectangular hole dug by neighbors in a corner of their farm. At that time, there were no funeral homes or mortuary services close by, so his family wrapped Kiptoo in a sheet and placed him in a home-made casket.

Their pastor led a brief prayer service, and the community surrounded the family as the sounds of grief filled the air, loud and wild. Swahili hymns were sung, not to silence the weeping and wailing, but to accompany it.

They lowered the casket six feet into the ground, and the dirt that had been dug out was thrown back in, hitting the wood of the casket with a distinct thud, thud, thud. This was a stinging yet hollow sound of finality. It reverberated in contrast to the words sung by the choir of neighbors about a land that is fairer than day, that by faith we can see it afar, for the Father is waiting and preparing a place to welcome us there.

* * *

While untimely death had robbed (some of) my children of their parents, it didn't rob them of their dreams. Like so many children, my kids' dreams of what they want to be when they grow up have ranged far and wide. On most days, Geoffrey will reliably tell you he wants to be an inventor. Ryan is convinced he will be a scientist. In fact, last year when he learned he was going to be an uncle at the age of five—an older biological sibling was having a baby—he cried and said, "Me don't wants to be an uncle. Me wants to be a scientist." Ella's goals have varied between becoming a professional tree climber and a veterinarian.

As for me, I didn't grow up with the goal of starting a hospice and funeral home in Kenya. Or of naming it Kimbilio, a place of shelter and refuge, and serving over one hundred thousand people a year from all over the country. I never imagined I would come to know the love of God in such profound ways because of this place and people, through the suffering and grief of many.

My office sits in between the hospice and funeral home. On one side, I can hear guests being pushed in their wheelchairs up the ramp to come for physical therapy. I can hear children's laughter as they walk to class with their teacher, Jacob. I hear the sounds of life.

From the other side, I hear buses and other vehicles arriving to pick up the bodies of their family members to take them home for burial. I hear sounds that accompany death—the familiar songs of funerals, as well as the long, loud, high-pitched cries of pain. When I hear these, I feel anguish in my belly, the tightening of discomfort in my chest.

Sometimes, the silence of death can be equally guttural.

As horrible as it is, there is something sacred about being able to grieve and lament together, within community. To believe that God is weeping with those who weep and inviting us to do the same.

Henri Nouwen wrote, "Do not hesitate to love and to love deeply. You might be afraid of the pain that deep love can cause... Every time you experience the pain of rejection, absence, or death, you are faced with a choice. You can become bitter and decide not to love again, or you can stand straight in your pain and let the soil on which you stand become richer and more able to give life to new seeds."[29]

---

29 Henri Nouwen, "Love Deeply," *Henri Nouwen Society,* February 3, 2023, https://bit.ly/3psJa2K.

Love invites us to be uncomfortable, to feel the weight of pain that others feel. And when we're hurting, others can help carry the weight of our pain, too.

I am convinced that where my office sits, as much as any place in the world, is like a bridge joining the space between life and death and what is to come. Being near to suffering and dealing with the physical, emotional, and spiritual aspects of death is rightfully hard. Sometimes, there is singing. Other times, there is silence as a guest takes their final breath. Some days, there is an unexplainable peace. Other days, there is great anguish.

I can imagine a whole host of guests who died here at Kimbilio—adults and children, whose names and stories our team remembers—welcoming, day by day, those who are joining them in heaven. No more pain, sorrow, sickness or death.

And what we cannot yet see, they now see in full.

* * *

I find the language and clichés around death and dying to be more troubling than the sounds of our fussy, dinosaur birds. We don't know what to say, so rather than be quiet, we resort to ha-da-da-like squawking, saying things like, "God must have needed another angel," "They're in a better place now," or "You loved them, but God loved them more."

To the last senseless comment, my unspoken response is always, "Really? God loved them more, so they had to die in such a horrible way?" That doesn't add up.

My least favorite is the language of replacement, especially to parents of a child who has just died. "There's still time. God will give you another child." As if one child can replace another.

Similarly, some strange language exists around sickness in many Christian circles. We pray for God to heal a person, convinced His will is always complete healing, even though every last one of us will die. But immediately after the person dies, we transition quickly to say, "They're in a much better place now with Jesus, where there is no sickness or death."

While all of this may be true, it's confusing to move so quickly from the certainty of healing to a resolution around death, instead of leaving room for the disappointment and the sadness of loss and grief. Why do we wrestle so insistently for healing now, if death is a better way? There needs to be room—space and time—for the sting of death and the pain of grief.

I was recently at a visitation in Eldoret, going through a slow procession line. I stood in front of a woman I had never met before, the sister of the person who had died. I hugged her and then remained awkwardly silent while I waited for the line to move. So I acknowledged the awkwardness, admitting that I didn't really know what to say, but I was so sorry for the death of her sister.

"Everyone keeps asking me, 'How are you?'" she responded. "I keep saying fine, but I am not fine."

I nodded as tears filled our eyes.

I don't think accompanying others through grief is about a specific timeline or "getting it right." Rather, it's about showing up and being willing to sit in silence, to feel the gravity of loss, to be uncomfortable. To help in practical ways when needed. To make a casserole or sift a pot of beans. To leave room for the messiness, for the tears that come when least convenient. To be careful how you position yourself in someone else's story of grief, or when and how you choose to give advice.

* * *

Shortly after arriving back in Kenya after our time in LA, I met a thirty-three-year-old mama at Kimbilio who was dying of an aggressive cancer. She was lying on a mattress in the shade of a tree, a broken mirror beside her. She picked it up often, checking to see if the dressing covering her face was still in place. To say her tumor was large and disfiguring does not begin to describe the extent of it. It filled her entire mouth and jaw, displacing her teeth and making it nearly impossible to swallow or speak. I knew breathing would soon be her next challenge.

Her mind was still intact, though, and she communicated by writing. As I knelt down beside her, she wrote with her blue pen on my hand the word *"ulimi,"* tongue. It was burning. And *"mzito,"* referring to the tumor being heavy.

Something about the words written on my hand felt familiar, not from the experience of a growing tumor but from the heaviness of suffering.

I couldn't hide from the weight of it as I sat next to Ryan during those December days in the ICU. Everything within me wanted him to live, but his survival didn't feel promised. As a machine breathed for him, the heaviness crushed my chest, too.

Mzito was a word I couldn't even articulate on those days when I had to remind myself to keep breathing, pleading, "Please let him live."

"I do not know any solace but to give ourselves into the love that will never cease to find us, that will never lose its hold on us, that will never abandon us to the sorrow for which it holds the cure," writes Jan Richardson.[30]

Mzito is inherent in the human condition of grief we all experience. Whether we can feel it or not, so is love. God is present with us in that heaviness, holding it with us.

---

30 Jan Richardson, *The Cure for Sorrow: A Book of Blessings for Times of Grief* (Orlando: Wanton Gospeller Press, 2016), 116.

To love and be loved.
Imperfectly. Wholeheartedly.
Making enough room
for all of you and all of me
to be welcomed and to belong.

Chapter Sixteen

Belonging

A letter to my life. This was the title that Njeri, a sixteen-year-old guest of Living Room, wrote not too long ago to begin a composition about her life's story. She penned the letter in her notebook and addressed it to me as "Dear Aunt," closing the letter with "Sincerely, your girl."

The sentences between those words were hard to read. They told of the hurt Njeri felt from being rejected by those who should have loved her, of being passed from one relative to another.

Her mother left. Her father drank. Her grandmother didn't want her. By the time Njeri was fourteen, she was working full-time as a maid in a stranger's home, caring for three small children. But then she became too sick to be useful.

Her words were piercing, telling of the grief she experienced watching her baby sister die of the same virus that had infected her since birth. In her words, HIV/AIDS equated "sickness, sadness, death."

Njeri arrived at Kimbilio Hospice terribly sick, too weak to walk or speak. A young girl in a little body, so broken by the world. Her concerns and troubles at sixteen seemed so cruel and hard to overcome. She came to us in need of physical care but also desperate for love and acceptance.

She needed to be told, with more than words, over and over again, that her life is significant, that her story matters. She needed a place of refuge and a people who would show her the love of God.

Day by day, life and strength are returning to Njeri. She is nearly ready to leave the hospice, and we are planning for her to stay close by, to begin school at a nearby boarding school. My prayer is that someday Njeri will be able to write another letter about her life, and the themes of rejection and loss will be replaced with redemption and unexpected joy.

* * *

In light of Njeri's courageous truth telling, I've been reflecting on my life and realized if I were to write a letter, it would likely be a series. For the season I'm currently in, I could tell of how I have been afforded the opportunity to grow and age, to get more fine lines and gray hair. To experience love and watch my hands gradually become like my mother's, as I learn to say "I don't know" a lot more than I used to.

For nearly fifteen years, I walked alongside mothers of chronically ill children as a nurse and patient-care advocate. I didn't know that, one day, I'd become a part of their club, the "Moms of Sick Kids" club—such a horrible title for a group that no one wants to be associated with. I'm sure there are better names: "No Thanks," "It's Too Much," or simply, "I Don't Want This."

For the past six years, though, I've been looking from the inside out and feel a kinship with other mothers walking similar paths. I still wish we could find our mutuality over something less heartbreaking and gut wrenching than the suffering of our children.

Our stories involve a willingness to go however far and to do whatever might be required for the love of our kids. And there doesn't seem to be another way except through it.

Alice experiences pain almost every day. She rarely complains about it, but it's in her body. It's in our home. And some days, it overwhelms her. There are daily medications to swallow and unanswerable questions about what treatment options might become available. There are follow-up appointments with lab results that remind us of misshapen blood cells that threaten her every organ. There are prayers that sound and feel a bit like a reminder of sorts: "Jesus, the one you love is sick."

Our boys no longer have sickle cell disease. What an indescribable gift it is to be able to say and have experienced that for five years now. Geoffrey and Ryan don't consciously remember the treatment or the pain they used to have, but their bodies have stored memories much like the scars etched upon their skin.

Every year, we travel to UCLA for follow-up appointments. These visits remind us of the gift of their lives, but they also come with reminders of the fear and trauma their treatment left within all of us. There is a long list of things to check on, to watch for. All of it unwanted, neatly fitting again into a "No, thank you" category.

Recently, these follow-up visits—the lab tests, eye exams, orthopedic evaluations, speech therapy, and more—have felt *mzito*, weightier than I expected. Not because it's all bad news. We have had plenty of days where that was true, and I am ever grateful for ongoing health. But there remains a chronicity to all of this.

I hold the wonder of their cure and an open-ended invitation to enjoy, but there are also triggers that remain, and the tension of scary unknowns still surround us.

The last few years have formed new depth within me, as I have moved from the host side of Living Room, the helper side, to the one needing help, the guest side. This shift has lent me compassion in ways I did not know before.

As I've been rethinking the story we often refer to as the Good Samaritan, I've been confronted, not by the question Jesus is asked: "Who is my neighbor?" I recognize what he's really addressing is this: Who do I have to love? Who do I have to extend mercy to?

And the question I am pondering is this: *Who am I in that story?*

I really want to be the one who notices another's suffering and cares enough to stop. The helper who recognizes the worth of the person who has been wronged.

I can also see myself as the religious person who talks about generosity and compassion but chooses to look away, to keep walking, for a host of reasons.

On any given day, I can identify with both these characters. They hold the power and privilege to choose whether to care or not.

The role I most struggle to imagine myself in is the person lying on the side of the road. The one beaten, victimized, and abandoned—desperate for someone to stop and help. Naturally, I don't want to be in this position. But I also wonder about the vulnerability that exists within all of us, as well as the systems of injustice and lived experiences, that make it more likely for some of us to be in that place and position than others.

I want to help and be helped when it is needed, to extend and receive mercy.

* * *

For a season, I felt like I had to divide myself between the roles of nurse and mother of children living with chronic illness. I didn't understand that in allowing these roles to blend, the vulnerability of being *both* could serve almost as a superpower.

It allows me to notice gaps that exist for patients, both within treatment as well as social determinants of health. It enables me to dig deeper into what holistic care could really look like.

I refuse to believe that my kids being sick is part of some divine plan to teach me a lesson, or that their suffering needs to make sense and add meaning to my life and work. That's not it. But it does prompt me to ask, *What does it look like to make choices from the lens of motherhood?*

This question—and its answers—feel closely linked to the original guiding question of my life and work: *What does it look like to love in this situation?*

How can we reimagine what healthcare can become if we focus on caring for a *person* and *family* unit rather than treating a *disease?*

Science and medicine are essential, but what are the other determinants that need to be considered within our daily practice?

I've always held a role of advocating for patients and their families. But as a mama, I feel the weight and importance of it at a whole new level. I can no longer look away from the barriers that keep people from accessing care, affording care, continuing within care.

I cannot ignore the cracks that are too wide, the gaps that delay service, the importance of determining the goals of care.

I have to consider more closely whether or not our communication is clear and kind in regard to diagnoses, treatment options, and prognoses.

I must also acknowledge barriers built within systems designed for the ease and convenience of providers, not patients. I must see the asymmetry of power, especially around the poor, when it comes to their health, their voice being heard, and outcomes.

The nurse and mother within me wants to support this journey, standing on the side of justice and mercy. Perhaps the Good Samaritan in Jesus's parable wasn't so much better than the others, as he was someone who better understood from his experience within the margins, his own solidarity with another in their suffering.

We are only able to recognize others' suffering when we begin to grasp that we truly need each other.

I didn't want to be a member of the "Moms of Sick Kids" club, but now that I belong, I find myself leaning in, bringing more of myself, as both mother and healthcare provider, to show up within my work. Recognizing, as I make room for the various parts of who I am, all of me gets to belong. The remarkable thing is, being fully myself invites others to belong in deeper ways, too.

Brené Brown captures this truth well, saying, "True belonging doesn't require you to change who you are; it requires you to be who you are."[31]

There is a humility in the tension of learning to be both host and guest, to keep showing up with a willingness to not get it perfect, but also a deep conviction, rooted and established in love, that gives me solid ground to stand on.

* * *

I had a dream one night, shortly after we arrived home from LA, about a guesthouse at Living Room in Eldoret. It was filled with children and families who'd traveled far distances to undergo cancer treatment at a nearby government hospital.

In the dream, I could feel the love and warmth, the beauty of the space. It was run by a Kenyan team, and it had a name: Micah's Guesthouse.

The guesthouse was extending the same type of welcome and kindness our family received. The name clearly represented Baba Micah, Mama Micah, and Micah, who had demonstrated such extravagant hospitality to my family.

---

31 Brené Brown, *Braving the Wilderness: The Quest for True Belonging and the Courage to Stand Alone* (New York: Random House, 2017), 40.

In my dream, along the doorpost of the guesthouse read the guiding message of Micah 6:8: "He has shown you what is good; And what does God require of you but to do justly, to love mercy, and to walk humbly with your God" (see Mic. 6:8).

Three years later, we built a sixty-four-bed guesthouse at Living Room and indeed named it Micah's Guesthouse. Each of the beds is covered with a turquoise blanket and a teddy bear made of bright, kitenge fabric—waiting to meet its new owner.

Living Room provides free food, accommodation, and daily transportation to and from the hospital for these families. Our team boils big pots of chai and makes enough *mandazi,* Kenyan pastries, in the morning to nourish these beloved little ones, to say to their mamas and daddies, "You are loved and worthy of it."

Each afternoon, a team of social workers, caregivers, and a teacher gather to tutor the kids, play games, color and sing, dance and make crafts.

Our prayer is that hospitality and love will make room for the possibility of healing for many of these children. We want all who come into our care to know they aren't alone as they walk this hard journey. Our desire is to partner with these families and the government hospital, filling the wide housing gap that makes it nearly impossible for them to complete treatment. It feels impossible to put into words just how beautiful and sacred this work is.

While the construction of this guesthouse was winding up, Baba and Mama Micah visited Kenya, arriving five years to the day since we had moved into their home. When they visited Living Room's hospital, we were already housing fifteen children, each with a guardian, and we all shared a lunch together.

At the end of the lunch, the sign, which had once only been a part of a dream but now was being lived out, was presented from the children to Mama and Baba Micah. In bold letters, it read, *Do Justly. Love Mercy. Walk Humbly.*

* * *

One morning, I stood at the top of the atrium overlooking the rooms still being constructed in the guesthouse. These would soon be filled with tired mamas and sick children. I could already see the space becoming a place where beauty and brokenness would sit, side by side. Where dancing and singing could live, as well as the heartache and sadness of what was today and what might come tomorrow. It felt familiar, like a place where I, too, had sat and wept and waited.

Soon, beautiful art created by local artisans would be hung overhead—quilts hung on the walls throughout the guesthouse and monarch butterflies and a rainbow of flowers hung overhead in the atrium. Life-sized sculptures of a brightly painted mother and baby giraffe would welcome all the children who enter.

I felt the weight of the room as well as the warmth of the sun. Around me, welders were still welding and painters, painting. A song I learned as a child rose within me. It stirred inside of me until I let it free, singing: "This little light of mine, I'm gonna to let it shine. This little light of mine, I'm gonna let it shine. Let it shine. Let it shine. Let it shine."

* * *

A few weeks after the guesthouse opened, a gospel choir from Nairobi came to visit. Before going into the building, a ten-year-old guest named Chemeli leaned against her mama so she could walk toward the music. Although she was weak from the treatment, as well as her advanced cancer, she wanted to sing, too.

When they reached the room from where the music came, Chemeli sat down next to her mom and requested her favorite song, her voice barely audible: *"Imba nashukuru Mungu."* Sing thank you, God. As the choir began to sing her song, Chemeli joined in. Her mom's tears flowed freely as she, too, sang along.

"To bless is to bridge," K.J. Ramsey writes. "A blessing is a bridge to belonging, built right in the place we feel separated from hope. Words of blessing bring us back to the beautiful truth of being human: we belong to one another, and it is in the space between our souls that we become strong."[32]

As the singing continued, I found myself swaying side to side, back and forth. It wasn't about the rhythm of the music as much as the quieting of my soul, a deep sense of the weight and the overwhelming love held within that sacred moment, weaving itself into a thousand other moments, choices, and memories.

---

32 K. J. Ramsey, *The Book of Common Courage: Prayers and Poems to Find Strength In Small Moments* (Grand Rapids, Zondervan, 2023), 11

To bless is to bridge.
With our words, our welcoming.
With our imagination and actions.
Making room for the beauty and
brokenness of this world, of our lives.
For the reminders that love is greater
than death, greater than our fears.
Showing up without hiding. Without apology.
I am here for you, and you are here for me.
For the hope of healing that hasn't yet come.
For giving thanks.
For permission to grieve our losses, failures,
disappointments.
For the shelter of community that has held us.
For the grace to keep unclenched
hands and open doors.
For the courage to know when it is enough.
When to rest. When to fight.
For the memorizing, lest we forget:
Only love matters.
We belong to one another.
And may our voices keep humming, singing into the
dark, "This little light of mine, I'm gonna let it shine."

You Are Invited

L ong before my family's transplant journey, I helped to create Living Room, a healthcare organization in Kenya where men, women, and children come either to heal or to be loved until they die.

As a healthcare worker, I know the importance of providing quality physical, emotional, and spiritual care to our patients every single day. As a mother who has walked the long and scary road of suffering with my own children, I understand even more intimately the impossible task every healthcare worker takes when they choose to love their patients and their patients' loved ones. I see even more clearly the cost of standing in the gap to offer hope, care, and advocacy for those in need.

At Living Room, our team of doctors, nurses, support staff and administrative staff walk alongside the patients and families going through medical crises. Committed to loving them and one another, through the good and bad days. If you are a healthcare worker, we want to walk alongside you too. This work is hard, and you are not alone.

To learn more about Living Room's loving work and ways you can get involved, please visit LivingRoomInternational.org.

I'd love to hear from you. You can reach me via email or Instagram:

juli@juliboit.com

@julimcgowanboit

@LivingRoomInternational

Acknowledgments

The stories that fill the pages of this book represent sacred relationships that have accumulated over nearly twenty years. I am deeply grateful for those, too numerous to name here, who have shared themselves so generously with me. Thank you for teaching me more about the ways of love.

Thank you to Brian and Krissy and the entire team at Hope*Books for making this book a reality. To Abby, Staci, and Adele, thank you for gifting this story with your remarkable editorial talents.

Thank you to Mel, Mary, and Micah for opening your home, hearts, and community to our family. We love you and will always be grateful.

To Mark, Tom, and our entire CA family, thank you for your commitment to love and generosity. I am thankful I get to be a follower of Jesus with you.

A great debt is owed to Living Room's leaders and staff whom I am honored to serve alongside. Thank you for choosing to show up each day and bravely love in such tangible ways. My gratitude to David and Allison Tarus and Living Room's Board of Directors. To all the guests and families who have entrusted us with their care, please know that Living Room exists for you. To Living Room's partners from around the globe, thank you for all of the ways you stand with us.

To the Boits and McGowans, thank you for your constant love and support.

And finally, to Titus and our children, my deepest love and most profound thanks goes to you.

About the Author

Juli Boit, author and nonprofit leader, operates at the intersection of faith, global health, and human dignity. Since 2004, she has resided and worked in Africa, founding Living Room International—a community-led nonprofit providing medical care in Kenya—and serving as its International Director.

As a Family Nurse Practitioner, Juli has united her dual passions for healthcare and social justice, fashioning a unique manifestation of love that delivers vital services to an underserved community. For additional information and booking, please visit juliboit.com.

Learn more at **juliboit.com.**

www.ingramcontent.com/pod-product-compliance
Lightning Source LLC
Chambersburg PA
CBHW060910120626
46553CB00001B/275